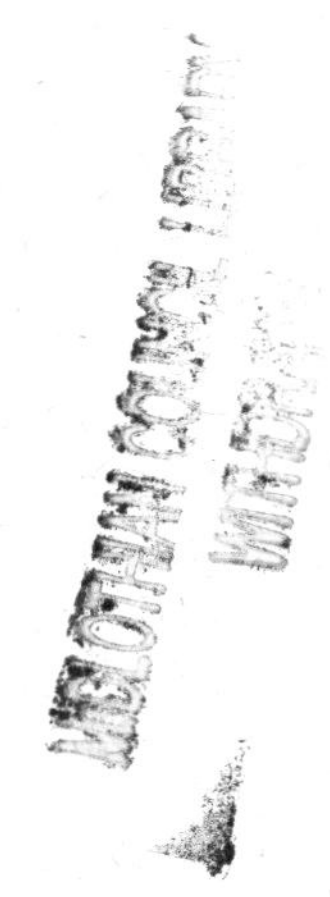

MONDRIAN

FRANK ELGAR

208 illustrations
41 in colour

TH AND HUDSON · LONDON

Translated from the French by
THOMAS WALTON

PRINTED IN FRANCE

Contents

Foreword

In any monograph on an artist, his life counts for less than his work. After all, the fact that nothing is known of the anonymous masters of the fourteenth and fifteenth centuries does not lessen our admiration for their painting. Mondrian resembles them in a way; although this theoretician of neo-plasticism was one of our contemporaries, and although his name is a famous one, he remains virtually unknown as a human being.

Even less is known of Mondrian today than of Seurat, that other great solitary; so I have not hesitated to draw heavily on the testimonies of those who did know and understand him. Chief among these is Michel Seuphor, who has abundantly documented the artist's whole career.

My debt to M. Seuphor is a major one. But it goes without saying that I have not hesitated, when it has seemed necessary, to put forward certain interpretations based on my own minute study of Mondrian. This freedom seems to me all the more justified in that without it there can be no honest approach to the works themselves.

FRANK ELGAR

1 *Self-portrait* *c.* 1900

CHAPTER ONE

The years of apprenticeship

The fate attending the ideas and work of Piet Mondrian, which have influenced not only the painting, but also the architecture, sculpture, decorative arts and even the fashions of the twentieth century, might give the impression that he was merely one among other pioneers of abstract art, or, more precisely, of the geometrical abstract art which came into such prominence in the years immediately following the Second World War. But Mondrian was much more than an innovator. By pursuing his quest resolutely to its conclusion, by discovering a universal order running through the world of his perception and experience, he first opened the way towards a new language of painting and then closed it again so completely that any subsequent advance in the same direction was rendered impossible.

As so often happens – as it happened in the case of another great Dutch artist, Vincent van Gogh – Mondrian's early efforts in no way forecast the trajectory of his subsequent career. Yet it was by inflexible logic that he was led from the naturalism of the Barbizon painters to the rigorous abstraction of his *Broadway Boogie-Woogie*. *Ill. 207*

Piet Mondriaan – that is the original spelling, with two a's – came from a lower middle-class Dutch family whose members included a fair number of draughtsmen and painters. But, as he himself said, 'not one of them would have agreed to sacrifice anything at all for art'. The eldest of a family of four boys and a girl, he was born on 7 March 1872. His father, a schoolmaster, was, he says, 'always drawing, but in his case it was no more than a pastime'. It was his uncle, Frits Mondriaan, a professional artist and former pupil of Willem Maris, who gave him his first lessons in painting.

Their father was an intransigent Calvinist, and so the Mondriaan children were brought up according to the strictest moral principles. Piet, being of a docile character, was unable to evade his father's domination. He had been drawing and painting since he was fourteen. Since his father had chosen a teacher's career for him, he decided to become a drawing-master and for several years he worked hard on his own to obtain the necessary diplomas. Then, having achieved that aim, he refused to begin the job. His father, realizing that the boy turned a deaf ear to all his remonstrances, finally gave way, and, through the good offices of a friend of the family, Piet was able to go to Amsterdam to study at the Academy of Fine Arts. That is how, in November 1892, he came to leave the little town of Winterswijk, where his family had settled in 1880. Still very much dominated by his father, Mondrian is said to have asked his permission to attend a life-class at the Academy.

THE NATURALIST PERIOD

Far from succumbing to the attractions of the big city, Mondrian proved to be a most assiduous student at the Academy where he began his three years' apprenticeship to painting. And when, at the end of that time, he had to turn to a number of different jobs in order to earn his living, he continued for another two years to attend drawing classes in the evenings. Besides the traditionalist example set by August Allebé, the Director of the Academy, he also came

2
urch Apse
c. 1892

under the influence of Breitner, the pupil of Jozef Israëls. Mondrian painted landscapes and still-lifes, always choosing the least picturesque, not to say the most unpromising subjects, and he painted staidly, stolidly and strictly according to academic rule.

In 1928 his sister Christien was to sell to a Breda collector one of Piet's charcoal drawings, *Stream in the Forest,* dated

1888. It is easy to see, in this work of extreme youth, the dominating influence of his masters, influenced in their turn by the French painters of the Barbizon school. But it was not long before Mondrian asserted greater freedom in his choice of criteria, so, although his *Boats in Moonlight* (1890) and his *Sheaves of Corn* (1891), or the two still-lifes, *Pot and Onions*
Ill. 3 and *Herrings and Lemons*, dated 1892 and 1893, show him still
Ill. 2 enslaved by Dutch naturalism, his *Church Apse* (*c.* 1892) is bathed in the light of Corot and the melancholy impressionism of Breitner. With these influences, the formulas of Théodore Rousseau and Millet also gave their individual accent to his *Washerwomen* (*c.* 1896), the *Landscape with*

3 *Herrings and Lemons* 1893

4 *Landscape with Houses and Canal* c. 1897

Houses and Canal (*c.* 1897), and to watercolours like the *Drydock at Durgerdam*. The hold which Breitner had over him was to give way to the influence of Jan Toorop, particularly noticeable in a symbolist painting of 1900 entitled *Spring Idyll,* which is all in half-tints, lightly applied and fluid to the point of evanescence. Having taken part in the activities of the Brussels group Les Vingt, Toorop was familiar with the work of the French symbolist poets and painters, as well as with that of the English Pre-Raphaelites and the Austrian artist Gustav Klimt. He absorbed and combined these different influences in an eclectic language which was taken up by the painters of the young Dutch school and which stimulated the researches of innovators like Van der Leck, Van Doesburg and, for a short while, Mondrian himself.

Ill. 4

Ill. 5

At this point in his career Mondrian had difficulty in making a living. In the autobiographical essay of 1942, *Towards the True Vision of Reality,* written in English, he says of this period: 'At twenty-two began a very difficult time for me. To make a living I did many kinds of works – bacteriological drawings for textbooks and schoolrooms, portraits, copies

5
Spring Idyll
1900

6 *Factory* 1899

of pictures in museums. And I taught as well. Then I began to sell landscapes. It was a hard struggle, but I managed to make a living and was glad to be able to earn just enough money to be able to do what I wanted to do.'

Mondrian had many points in common with his compatriot Vincent van Gogh. Although he never suffered hunger and poverty to the extent that Van Gogh did, he too had to choose between the same conflicting vocations, art and religion, and face the same stiff-necked Calvinism in his family. Mondrian, like Van Gogh, had crucial mystical experiences, but these were to resolve themselves with the study of theosophy. Even his painting, at least as he practised it until the age of thirty, shows similarities with the painting of Van Gogh's Dutch period. But there the similarity ends. For

7 *Mill by the Water* c. 1900

although the Latin south brought sudden enlightenment to Van Gogh, it left Mondrian completely unmoved. In 1901 he returned from a trip to Spain with a painter friend, Simon Maris, the son of Willem Maris, filled with disappointment and more than ever attracted to the light, the things and the people of his native Holland.

A visit to England made shortly after his return was also unprofitable. However, the few weeks he spent in Brabant in August 1903 with Albert van den Briel, a young student he had met in Amsterdam in 1899, were so pleasant that he decided to go and live there. In January 1904 he went to Uden where he rented a cottage, No. 29 Sint Janstraat. Uden was a village surrounded by farms, pastureland, windmills; these were to become his favourite themes. His contacts with the local peasantry, whose rough manner and simple Catholic faith he found congenial, also helped him to readjust his vision. His painting at this period is correspondingly bold and vigorous. His colours are dark, harsh and gloomy, but enlivened, when he is searching for crepuscular effects, with mauves and blues.

Van den Briel lived not far away, at Hilvarenbeek, near the Belgian border. Mondrian visited him there, and his friend often came to Uden where they exchanged ideas on art, religion and philosophy which were the product of anxiety more often than of certitude.

8
Autumn Landscape
c. 1902

9
Woods near C
c. 1907

10 *Landscape* 1907

REALIST THEMES

By the end of a year Brabant had lost its attraction. Mondrian returned to Amsterdam where, from 22 February 1905 to 28 June 1906, he had a studio at 10 Rembrandtplein. From there he moved to 272 Albert-Cuypstraat. In Amsterdam he renewed his contacts with Simon Maris and made friends with another painter, Albert Hulshoff. Until 1906, he was still finding inspiration in and around the capital, on the banks of the Amstel and the Gein, as well as in the picturesque hamlet of Oele, where he rented a room in the house of the village schoolmaster. Rustic cottages, windmills, polders, barges, trees leaning over still water were the subjects that appealed to him. But, as he became still more and more attentive to light, more and more responsive to the charm of French painting as revealed to him by Toorop and Jan Sluyters, Mondrian began to bring wide perspectives into his pictures, lowering the horizons, broadening the skies and filling them with the warm tones produced by the setting sun.

After *The Amstel, Evening Impression, Pond near Saasveld* and *Sheepfold at Evening,* all dating from 1907, he painted, in
Ill. 12 the following year, an *Evening Sky* that is a radiant mass of
strong, fresh colours. But he returned to a much more deli-
Ill. 10 cately shaded palette in his paintings of moonlight: *Landscape*
(Stedelijk Museum, Amsterdam), *Trees on the Banks of the*
Ill 14 *Gein at Moonrise* (Gemeentemuseum, The Hague).

The variety of these attempts must not be allowed to mislead us. Mondrian was far from being eclectic. We find

11
Sketch for Landscape near Oele
c. 1907

12 *Evening Sky* 1907–8

him, from now on, returning incessantly to the same themes, working on them in depth and with countless variations, as if he were searching not so much for himself as for a certain way of representing the real, and of expressing, already at this early date, its quintessence. Two series of canvases, the *Farm at Duivendrecht* (1906–7) and the *Trees on the Banks of the Gein* (1907–8) are evidence of this preoccupation. Sometimes swathed in a mist that softens all its details, sometimes striped with broad, sweeping strokes of ultramarine, golden yellow, emerald green, and mauves and violets, the subject becomes, in the end, unrecognizable. Curiously enough, this does not

Ill. 18
Ills 13–14

13 *Trees on the Banks of the Gein at Moonrise* 1907–8

Ills 19–21 occur in the *Chrysanthemum* series, started in 1906 and followed
by other flower studies – marigolds, dahlias, rhododendrons,
Ill. 22 sunflowers.

Over a period of some ten years Mondrian was to return, at intervals, to the flower motif, as if he had never succeeded in mastering its challenge. Each flower is represented singly, neither freshly opened nor yet in full bloom, but, in most cases, when life seems to be ebbing from it, as in the *Dying*
Ill. 21 *Chrysanthemum* (Gemeentemuseum, The Hague), dated
1907–8. By choosing either autumn flowers such as chrysanthemums, or other flowers about to fade, Mondrian may have

14 *Trees on the Banks of the Gein at Moonrise* 1907–8

wished to symbolize the inevitability of decay and death. Bearing in mind his natural propensity for metaphysical thought, this is certainly possible. The lilies and amaryllis he sent to the exhibition organized in 1910 by the Sint-Lucas Society in Amsterdam are handled more firmly, though the rendering is still superficial. In his autobiographical essay Mondrian wrote: 'I was always a realist . . . I disliked particular movement, such as people in action. I enjoyed painting flowers, not bouquets, but a single flower at a time.'

His nudes are few in number; with only rare exceptions, he did not paint nudes after 1905. The large triptych entitled

Evolution (*c.* 1911), which is decadent in its symbolism and mediocre in its execution, and two studies dated 1912, both clumsily cubist in manner, were no more than isolated experiments. Such portraits as he did were obviously painted to order. 'My environment conditioned me to paint objects of ordinary vision; even at times to make portraits with likeness. For this reason much of this early work has no permanent value.' There is no denying his portraits were a mistake. His self-portraits are little better, though worthy of attention for their documentary value. In his 1900 and 1908 portraits we
Ill. 1 see him with high forehead and blazing eyes, and with a beard and moustache (Phillips Gallery, Washington, and Slijper
Ill. 46 Collection, Blaricum). Two charcoal drawings dated 1911 and 1912 show him three-quarter face, clean-shaven, revealing a strong, determined chin and stressing the sharp curvature of the nose. The difference between the two groups is striking. Whereas the first two self-portraits reveal an artist still on the

15 *The Amstel River, Evening Impression* 1907

16 *The River Amstel in the Evening* c. 1907

fringes of society, still vulnerable to the doubts and the fevers of youth, the later ones put before us a man who has made his way and, having found his place in the world and put on a jacket and tie, is all the more fully aware of the price one pays for certitude. Apart from the imprints which age was to make upon it, it is already the face that would be familiar, years later, to his friends in Paris or New York.

But the metamorphosis had not yet taken place, and his painting was still thoroughly steeped in Dutch naturalism. Everything about him made that inevitable – his conservative temperament, his family upbringing, the advice of his uncle Frits, who had been his first mentor, the influence of the Hague painters such as Mauve, the Maris brothers and

Weissenbruch, followed by that of the Amsterdam 'impressionists', including Israëls and Breitner. The term 'impressionist' was really justified only by their opposition to the descriptive realism of the painters of the Hague school, who liked to think of themselves as the heirs of the Barbizon school, by the greater freedom of their brushwork and also by the interest they showed in light and painting in the open air. Even then, it must be quite clear that, while Mondrian could admire these masters, then universally recognized, he never worked under the direction of any one of them. In fact, he remained for a long time unaware of the aesthetic upheavals that had been taking place in France during the previous forty years. The little he did learn aroused in him not the slightest desire for further knowledge. Uninvolved and unambitious

17 *Farm at Duivendrecht* before 1908

18 · *Farm at Duivendrecht* c. 1908

as he was, all he cared about was accomplishing his self-imposed task in peace. He could not therefore be expected to denounce the violation of independence. He was not basically interested in revolution. Revolutionary truth was to reveal itself to him slowly, only with the passage of time. And when he did at last embrace it, it was without ostentation, without anger, but with inflexible determination.

A general survey of Mondrian's paintings up to 1908 makes it easy to recognize their strict, studied, commonplace realism. They are even inferior to the paintings of his older contemporaries, whose influence he acknowledged. Van Gogh in his naturalist phase had shown both greater ability and deeper inspiration. Even Van der Leck, who also eventu-

19
Chrysanthe
c. 1908–10

ally forswore realism, has left works which Mondrian might have envied. This is not altogether surprising, for some of the greatest masters did not find their vocation or feel the touch of genius until late in life. 'The man who has not realized

21 *Dying Chrysanthemum* 1908

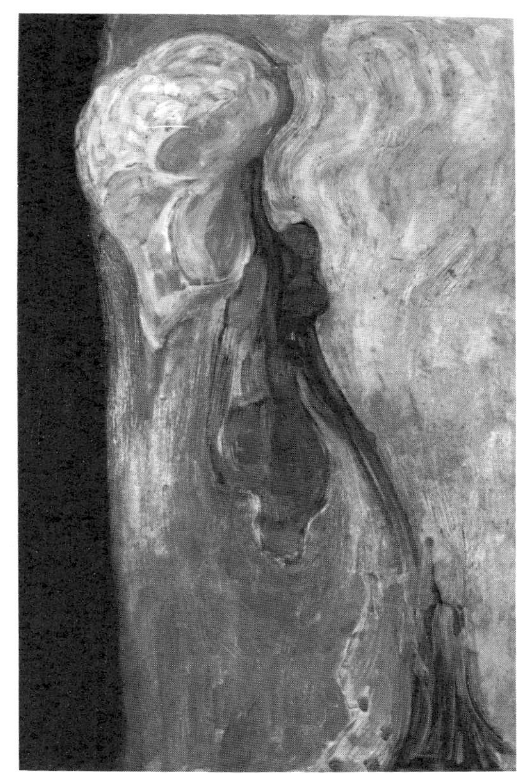

20 *Dying Chrysanthemum* *c.* 1907

the difficulty of art', said Chardin in 1765, 'never does anything worth while; the man who realized it too soon does nothing at all.'

Mondrian lived in a very closed circle, with no opening to

22 *Dying Sunflower*
1907–8

23
Tiger Lily
1909

the world outside. There was no *avant-garde* at that time in Holland. Van Dongen was already in Paris. Sluyters was travelling through Europe. True, there was Floris Verster and, especially, Jan Toorop, who were propagating symbolism in their native country. But Mondrian was to have no regular contact with Toorop until after 1908. Up to then his naturalism was scarcely affected by new ideas. In his autobiography, he said of this period: 'After several years, my work unconsciously began to deviate more and more from the natural aspects of reality. Experience was my only teacher; I knew little of the modern art movement. When I first saw the work of the impressionists, Van Gogh, Van Dongen and the fauves, I admired it. But I had to seek the true way alone.'

CHAPTER TWO

From cubism to abstraction

In 1908 Mondrian first began to be aware of the path he was to follow; it was the year that marked a turning point in his development. He went with his friend Cornelis Spoor to spend the summer at Domburg, a village tucked away in the dunes on the island of Walcheren, in Zeeland. In the next seven years, he was to return there many times. It was at Domburg that he became involved with the group of young artists led by Toorop. Toorop was fifty, Mondrian thirty-six. A close friendship soon developed between the two painters, particularly because Toorop's mysticism was

24
Hayricks
c. 1909

25 *The Red Cloud* 1907

naturally congenial to Mondrian's theosophical leanings. (Later, everything Mondrian had discovered in his friend's painting – symbolist statements, impressionist tendencies – he found repellent.) Furthermore, Sluyters, whom he had known at the Amsterdam Academy, had come back from Paris markedly influenced by fauvism. His admiration for Matisse, Derain, Vlaminck and, through them, Van Gogh, who was still unappreciated in his native country, was evident. It is likely that Sluyters tried to persuade Mon-

26 *Woods near Oele* 1908

drian to share his new convictions. At any rate, before he had close friendships with either Toorop or Sluyters, Mondrian had seen their work at exhibitions in Amsterdam in which the one acknowledged his debt to Pissarro's and Seurat's use of light, and to the mannerism of the Nabis, and the other his debt to the brutal sensualism of the French fauves.

TRANSITION

The first picture in which Mondrian tried to alter his tech-
Ill. 26 nique seems to have been a landscape, *Woods near Oele* (Gemeentemuseum, The Hague), painted in 1908 in his

27
Lighthouse at Westkapelle
1910

Amsterdam studio, in a range of pure tones applied with broad, rapid brushstrokes. He used the same technique in the *Ruined Castle at Brederode*, a subject treated by Hobbema in the seventeenth century. These two canvases, with other works by Mondrian, were shown in an exhibition which opened in January 1909 at the Stedelijk Museum, Amsterdam. The two other artists represented were Sluyters and Cornelis Spoor. The critics greeted this show with an icy reception, sharply attacking Mondrian in particular. His Brabant pictures found favour, but the others, the ones he

28
Windmill in Sunlight
c. 1911

had most recently painted with restrained audacity, were ridiculed. 'Unfinished', 'raving mad', 'unbalanced' were a few of the epithets applied to them. They nevertheless attracted the attention of W. Steinhoff, the art critic who

Ill. 24 gave a carefully judicious account of the three *Hayricks* (1908) in the *Amsterdammer* of 31 January 1909: 'One', he

29 *Church-Tower in Zouteland* 1910

30
The Red Mill
1910–11

wrote, 'is a blaze of colours under the blood-red rays of the declining sun; in another, paler, more subdued tints are bathed in the rosy glow that follows sunset, while in the third ghostly silhouettes stand out against a clear sky in the moment before nightfall.'

31
Church Tower at Domburg
1910–11

Indeed, soon after Mondrian arrived in Domburg he had painted, in the pointillist manner, some hayricks. These paintings have obviously much in common with those of Monet, in spite of the fact that he could have known them only by hearsay, or maybe through reproductions. This

32 *The Red Tree* 1909–10

Ill. 28 impressionism is more marked in the *Windmill in Sunlight* (1911; Gemeentemuseum, The Hague), with its flaming vermilions and strident yellows spattered with tiny points of vivid, pure colour. The same method is used in several pic-
Ill. 29 tures painted in 1910 of the *Church Tower in Zoutelande* and
Ill. 27 the *Lighthouse at Westkapelle,* which he had already painted the year before, though in a quite different manner. It appears, then, that in 1909 Mondrian was completely converted to a form of expression which owed as much to fauvism as to impressionism, and so we find him turning out a number of paintings and drawings based on the same set of motifs – the windmill and the church at Domburg, the lighthouse at Westkapelle, the church at Zoutelande, the

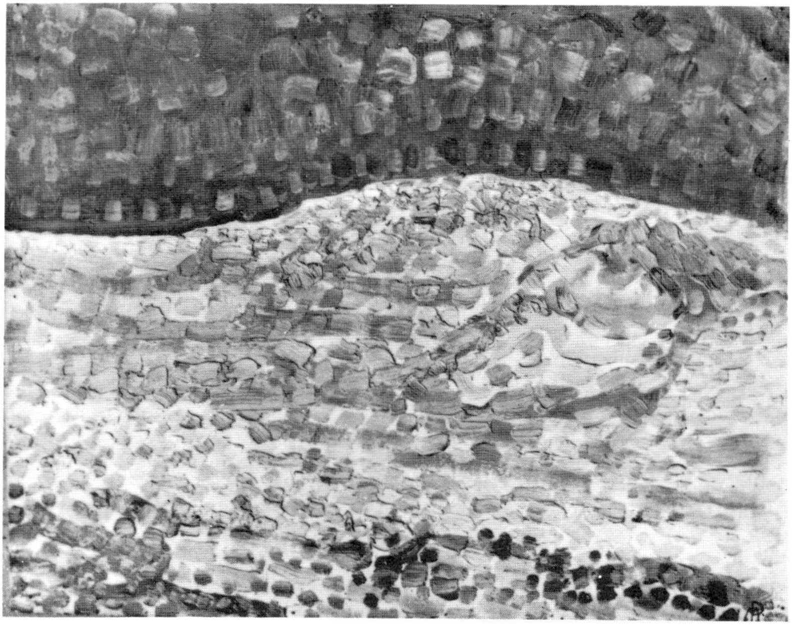

33
Dune
c. 1910

34
Dune
c. 1910

dunes and the sea in which he had discovered a daily spectacle ceaselessly renewed. These subjects he treated sometimes in the divisionist manner, sometimes by flat applications of cold and tenuous tones, as if he were hesitating between the vibratory style of Monet and the synthesism of the Nabis to which he had been introduced by Sluyters.

It was about this time, however, that Mondrian entered into direct and personal contact with the Paris school, through the exhibition organized in Amsterdam in October 1911 by the Moderne Kunstkring (Modern Art Circle), an association founded by the art critic Conrad Kickert. Kickert had been an ardent supporter of Mondrian since 1907 and prevailed upon him to join the association as a director-member with Toorop and Sluyters. The exhibition included, as well as pictures by the young Dutch school, among them some by Mondrian, nearly thirty canvases by Cézanne, and work signed by the most renowned French fauves and cubists. The following year a second exhibition brought together, in this case to pay tribute to Gauguin, the 'action group' of French painting, as well as recent works by Mondrian, including

35
Dunes and Sea
1909

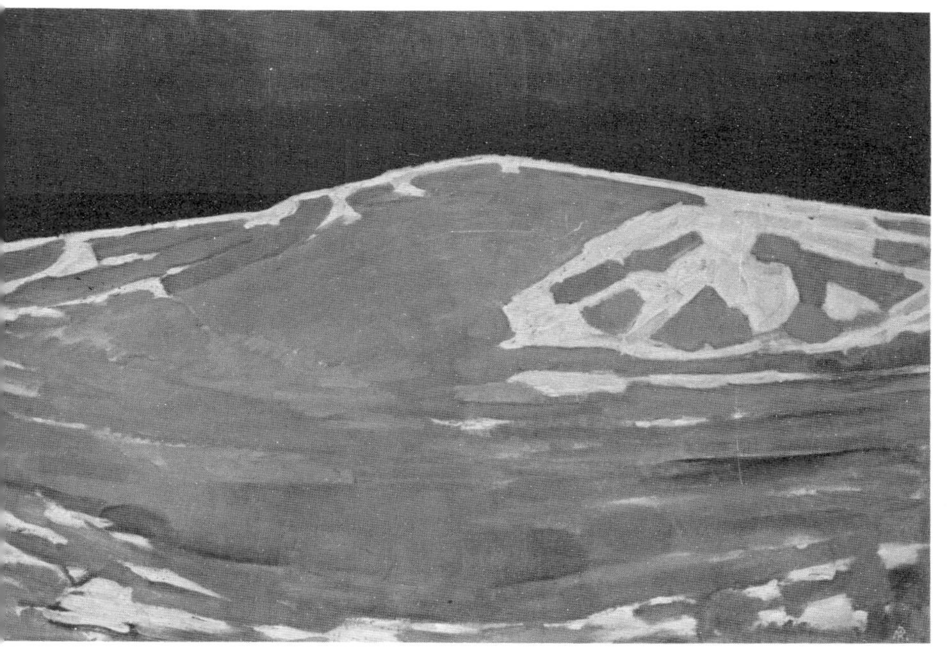

36 *Dune V* 1909–10

several of the famous *Trees* series. It is well to make it clear at this point that Mondrian was still, at this time, contributing to other collective exhibitions, such as the Sint-Lucas Society's exhibition of 1910, the Paris Salon des Indépendants of 1911 and, in the same year, a show at Domburg with the Walcheren group of artists led by Toorop. This last exhibition gave him the opportunity to show several versions of the *Dunes* theme. *Ills 37–44*

Mondrian had begun work on the *Trees* series in 1908, and its importance in the evolution of his art can never be overstated. The first picture in this series was of an apple-tree with widespread branches: *Red Tree* (Gemeentemuseum, *Ill. 32*

37 *Tree*
c. 1909–10

38 *Trees*
c. 1911

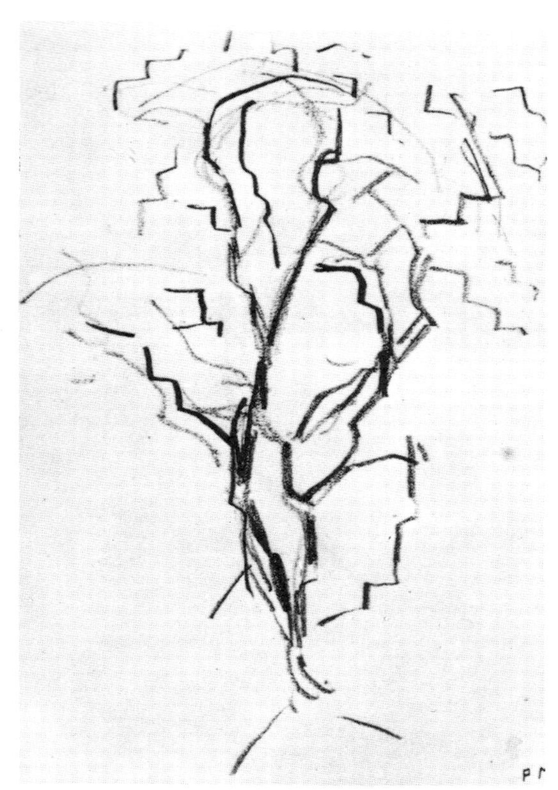

39 *Tree* c. 1911

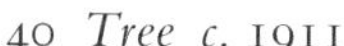

40 *Tree* c. 1911

41 *The Grey Tree* 1912

The Hague). The drawing was expressive, the colour non-naturalistic. It is the same tree he went on tirelessly reproducing, each time varying the colour and simplifying the form, becoming more and more abstract until, by 1912, it had been reduced, first to the skeletal structure of the model, and finally to a purely linear rhythm. The trunk became no more than a vertical axis, around which branches were indicated by a tangle of broken, repeated horizontal lines. Thus, the fundamental element of the doctrine of neo-plasticism, based on the relationship of vertical and horizontal
Ill. 37 lines, was already foreshadowed. Between the first *Tree*, markedly expressionist, and the last, progressively schematized, there is all the distance that separates reality from its quintessence, form seen from form imagined, the gulf that

42 *Tree* 1911

separates Van Gogh from a cubist like Braque or Picasso.

This critical period in the development of Mondrian's art, which began in 1908, reached a culminating point in 1911. Now he was a new man, determined to make the fact as clear to the rest of the world as it was to himself. He shaved off his moustache and beard. He modified the spelling of his name, no longer signing his work MONDRIAAN but MONDRIAN. Disclaiming his past, he decided to abandon naturalist illusionism and the accepted elements of painting: perspective, modelling, chiaroscuro. What precise form his own art was to take he did not yet know. But at least, by having swept all else away, he was able to see the path that was to lead him towards it. And that path – he was no longer able to persuade himself otherwise – ran through Paris.

43 *Composition with Trees* 1912

44 *Tree* 1912

Mondrian left Amsterdam and the studio he had rented at 42 Sarphatipark, probably on 20 December 1911. In Paris he settled in Montparnasse, in a studio at 26 Rue du Départ lent him by Kickert, who had used it as a *pied-à-terre* since 1909. It was there that Mondrian completed the *Trees* series.

Paris was at that time in a state of artistic turmoil. The memory of the impressionists and the fauves was still very much alive. The merits of Cézanne, Gauguin, Van Gogh and Seurat were no longer in dispute. Claude Monet and Auguste Renoir were ending their careers in a blaze of glory, while Kupka and Delaunay were already painting their first non-figurative compositions. It was the period of Fernand Léger's *Contrasts of Forms* and the proclamations of

45 Mondrian's studio, 26 Rue du Départ, Paris

46 *Self-portrait* 1911

Guillaume Apollinaire; the Section d'Or had just been founded and the first futurist exhibition had been held. Cubism was at last moving from its analytical to its synthetic period. It is difficult today to imagine the fever of invention and experiment which made the Paris of that time the living capital of the world of art.

It was into the midst of all this activity that Mondrian found himself suddenly plunged. Beset by so many temptations, what direction was this artist, with his logical and austere mind, going to take? By the intellectual character of their vision, the severity of their method, the discipline to which they submitted themselves in order to substitute for visible reality a reality conceived by the mind, it was to the cubists – Braque and, particularly, Picasso – that he found himself irresistibly attracted. He adopted their way of thinking, and with it their technique. Like them, he gave drawing priority

47 *Nude Study* 1912

48 *Sunflowers* 1912–13

over colour. He made their postulate his own: return to the idea and the object. But he quickly modified the latter term.
Ills 52–3 Indeed, if we except the two versions of the *Still-Life with Ginger Pot* (1912, Gemeentemuseum, The Hague), a *Female*
Ill. 49 *Nude* and a few secondary works, it soon became clear that

49
Female Nude
c. 1912

the object was destined to disappear. This also applies, as we have seen, to the *Trees* series, for he had soon reduced the object to a network of lines and tints – greys, as neutral as possible – arranged horizontally or vertically around a central focal point. He reduced his expression to the simplest

Ills 37–44

50 *Composition No. 1 (Trees)* 1912

possible terms, eliminated details, minimized the range and intensity of his colours and retained nothing of the subject but the lines of force, the internal structure, suggesting it by linear rhythms alone. In the rectangular format, which he continued to use, or in the oval format, the advantages of

51 *Oval Composition, Sketch* 1913

which he discovered in 1912, the works of his Parisian period are always distinguished by their moderate abstraction and their graphic, rather than pictorial, character: *The Grey* *Ill. 41*
Tree (1912, Gemeentemuseum, The Hague), *Tree* (1912, *Ill. 44*
Museum of Art, Carnegie Institute, Pittsburg).

Because he was older than the Parisian cubists, more cerebral, more instransigent, and far less of a sensualist, Mondrian was able to go beyond their limits and, by aiming only at subordinating line and colour to the surface and its division, to break the last bonds which held cubism to reality. Guillaume Apollinaire, always on the look-out for something new, had noticed the Dutch artist's contributions to the 1913 Salon des Indépendants. By bringing his readers' attention to 'the very abstract cubism of Mondrian' (he added that it was taking a quite different line from the cubism of Picasso and Braque) Apollinaire gave a precise definition of this experimental artist's work, still unknown to the public and even to his immediate neighbours, the habitués of Montparnasse.

52
Still Life with Ginger Pot I
1911

53 *Still Life with Ginger Pot II* 1912

Nearly all the cubists, including Gleizes, Metzinger, Léger, Reth, Serge Ferat, lived in Montparnasse. Picasso had left Montmartre to settle, first in the Boulevard Raspail, then in the Rue Schoelcher. But Mondrian seems to have made no contact with them. He lived in isolation in the Rue du Départ, working hard in spite of the non-stop clatter of trains and the round-the-clock activities of the local prostitutes and their clients. He was never seen at the Dôme or the Rotonde, the cafés favoured by Modigliani, Soutine, Archipenko, Zadkine, the gathering-ground of Bohemian artists, poets and revolutionary exiles. The thought of it

54 *Composition No. 7* 1913

repelled him, though one of his own pupils, a young Englishwoman, was a colourful figure among the dubious clientele of the Montparnasse cabarets. Flanked by an excessively corpulent Dutchwoman, she went about, summer and winter, dressed as a jockey. There is, however, no indication that Mondrian approved of his pupil's eccentricities.

The great city, from which he seems to have demanded, among many other things, a studious retreat, was to suggest to him a theme in perfect harmony with his immediate pre-

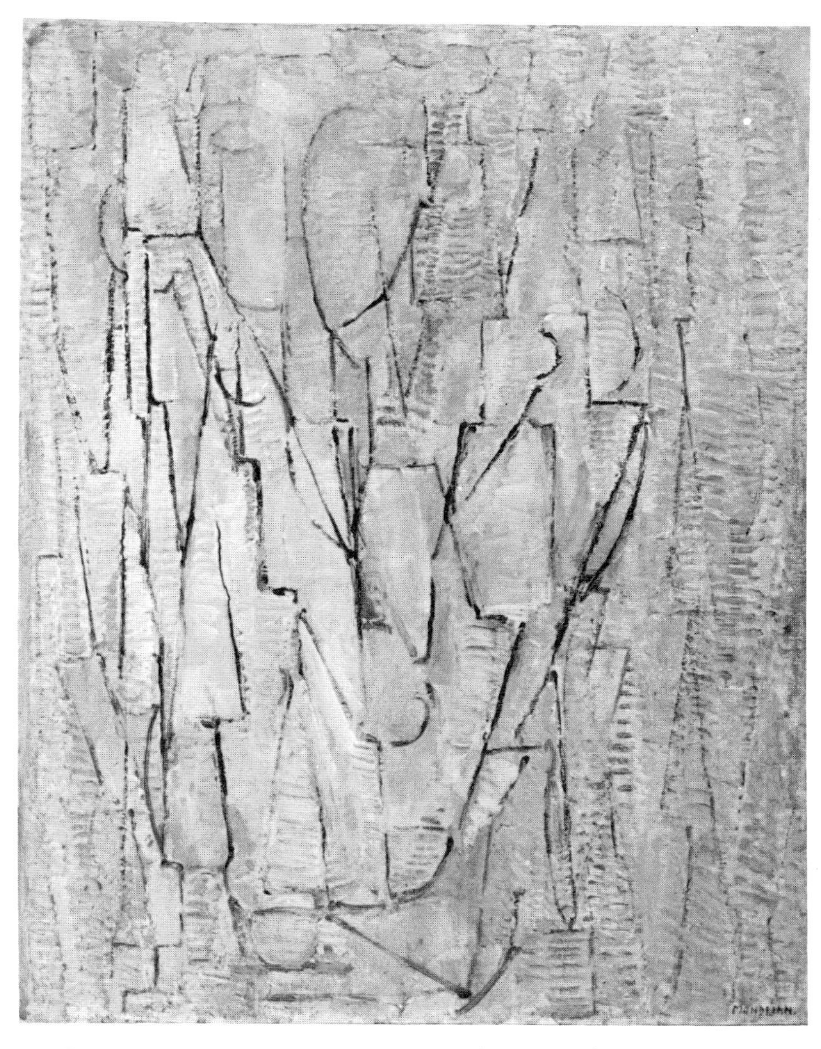

55 *Composition No. 11 c.* 1912

occupations, the theme treated in the two series, *Scaffolding* *Ill. 71*
and *Façades*. Inspired by the patterns of the façades of Parisian *Ills 61, 63–4*
buildings, especially when encased in scaffolding, he began a series of studies which, between 1912 and 1914, became

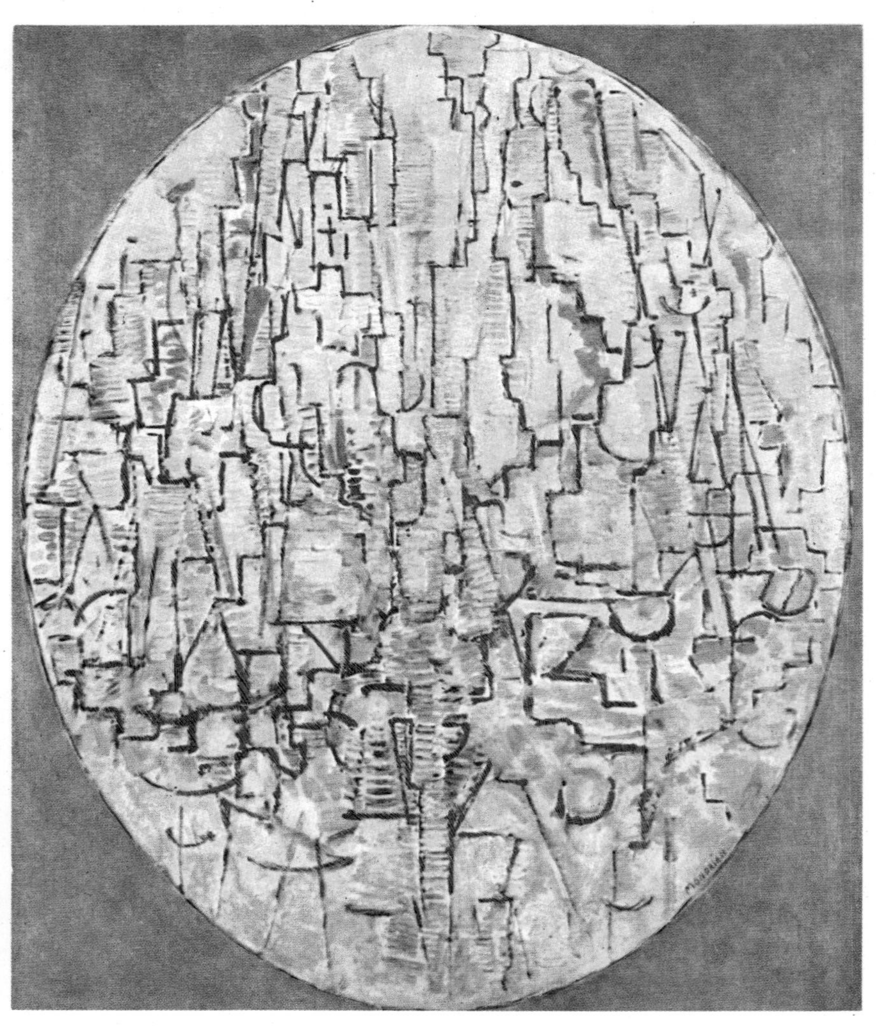

56 *Oval Composition (Trees)* 1913

diminishingly realistic, allusions to the original subject growing less and less explicit until, in the end, they were no more than geometric planes irregularly assembled and highlighted by only a few bright colours. To make the sense of

57 *Tableau I* 1913

58 *Scaffolding* c. 1912

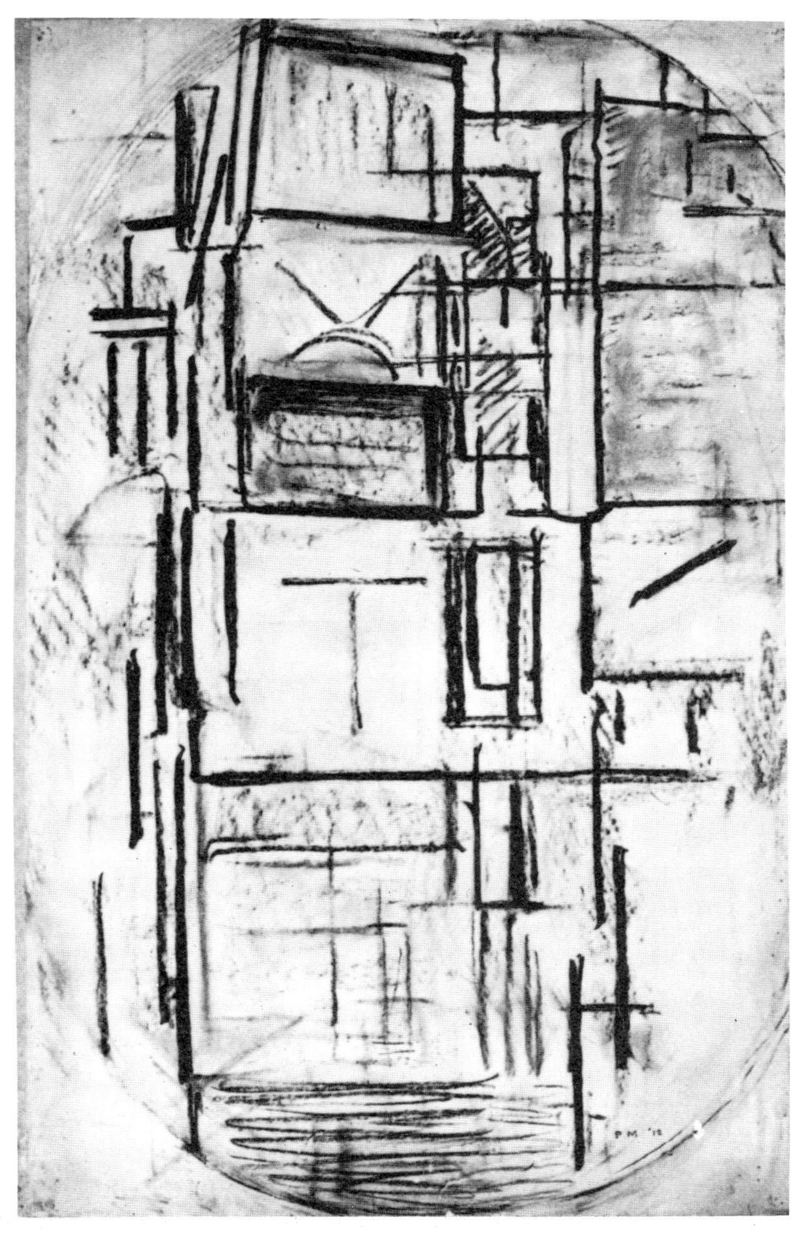

59 *Oval Composition (Sketch)* 1912

60 *Composition in Blue, Grey and Pink* 1913

this change quite clear, and to eliminate all reference to the outside world, Mondrian ceased, around 1912–13, to give his works conventional descriptive titles and began to identify them either by numbers – *Composition No. 1*, *Composition No. 2*, *Composition No. 3* – or by brief indications of colours and
Ill. 62 forms – *Oval Composition*, *Composition in Grey and Yellow*,
Ill. 75 *Oval Composition with Bright Colours*, *Composition in Blue*,
Ill. 60 *Grey and Pink*. All these canvases look almost like mosaics formed by straight lines crossing at right-angles. They would be boring were it not for the curves and the delicate greys which subtly break their monotony.

CHAPTER THREE

Prelude to neo-plasticism

At the beginning of August 1914 Mondrian was called to his sick father's bedside at Arnhem. (His father died the following year.) Caught unawares by the outbreak of war, he was forced to spend the next five years in his native country. Soon he was back again in Amsterdam, and then in Zeeland, where he renewed old friendships, particularly with Toorop. For a time, the painter who in later life proved sensitive to

61 *Façade No. 7* 1914

62 *Composition in Grey and Yellow* 1914

nature only in an industrial setting, was once more drawn to the poetry of the sea, the dunes, the ancient churches of Domburg and Zoutelande. Now, however, he interpreted such nature themes in his latest style, combining straight lines and curves in an architectural space in which colour seems, when not eliminated entirely, to serve only as an added attraction.

We are now far removed from the romantic works in which, five years previously, Zeeland landscapes and buildings were represented in a splash of yellows and vermilions. The interval had brought the revelation of cubism : the façades and scaffolding of Paris had produced graphic and chromatic effects of undeniable originality. Henceforth, Mondrian was to treat the subjects he chose with increasing boldness. In the early *Church Façades,* it is easy to identify the church at *Ill. 64* Domburg, suggested by its elevation, the ogive of its porch, *Ill. 65* its bays. The later works are nothing more than flowing networks of lines. The sea, which he had represented in 1912 by sinuous arabesques, he now interpreted by horizontal lines, first cut at each end by very short verticals, then later by tiny cross-bars, and finally, in 1917, by simple crosses and a scattering of short black lines grouped together inside an oval on a white ground *(Composition with Lines,* Kröller-Müller Museum, Otterlo). *Ill. 78* There are a number of works entitled *Piers and Ocean,* all composed with the same linear *Ills 72–4* motifs, which preceded this ultimate version. And one

63 *Façade in Brown and Grey* 1913

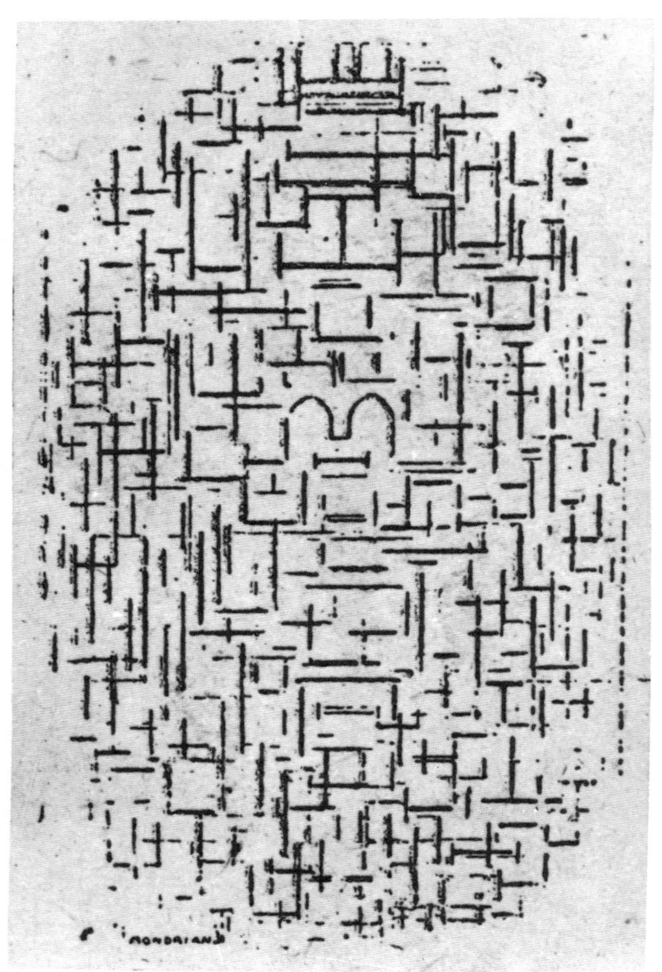

64
Church Façade
1914

finds the same cruciform signs, though less systematically
Ills 64–5 used, in several of his *Church Façades*, particularly in one on a
Ill. 80 grey ground dated 1916 (Solomon R. Guggenheim Museum, New York).

How did Mondrian arrive at such a concise and economical style? He reduced by half the outlines of the rectangular

65
Church at Domburg 1914

planes he had superimposed on each other in his earlier compositions. But, however simple the end result appears to be, it is infinitely less so when one considers the spirit of the work, obviously the outcome of an involved intellectual process. Indeed, we see in this juxtaposition of swarms of crosses the vertical-horizontal scheme which Mondrian was to make the

66
The Sea
c. 1914

67
The Sea
1913–14

68 *The Sea* 1914

69
The Sea
c. 1914

70
Composition with Colour Planes 1914

inviolable axiom of neo-plasticism. From this point onwards, he was to see nothing else in the world but perpendiculars and geometric surfaces: never volumes. To charge such elementary signs with such significance demanded from Mondrian much more than reasoning and logic. It demanded a profound love of the sea and the ability to respond intimately to its elemental power. And indeed Mondrian loved the sea

1 *Composition No. 9. Scaffolding* c. 1913

72
Pier and
1914

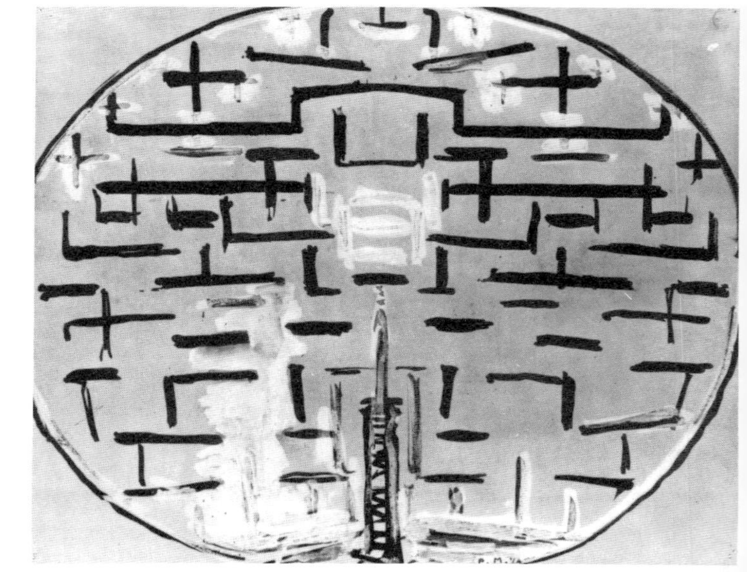

73
Pier and Ocean
1914

74 *Pier and Ocean* 1915

so dearly that he is said to have wanted, at the point of death, to see it once again. He was not, then, the implacable enemy of nature he was reputed to be, a fact made clear by the lines he was to write much later, in 1942: 'Observing sea, sky and stars, I sought to indicate their plastic function through a multiplicity of crossing verticals and horizontals. Impressed by the vastness of nature, I was trying to express its expansion, rest and unity. Perhaps that is why an art critic called one of these pictures "Christmas".' But the great surprise lies elsewhere; Mondrian goes on to accuse himself of having behaved at this period like an 'impressionist', more anxious to express a personal feeling than to describe reality itself.

Ills 66–9

75 *Oval Composition with Bright Colours* 1913

76 *Composition No. 6* 1914

77 *Composition* *c.* 1916

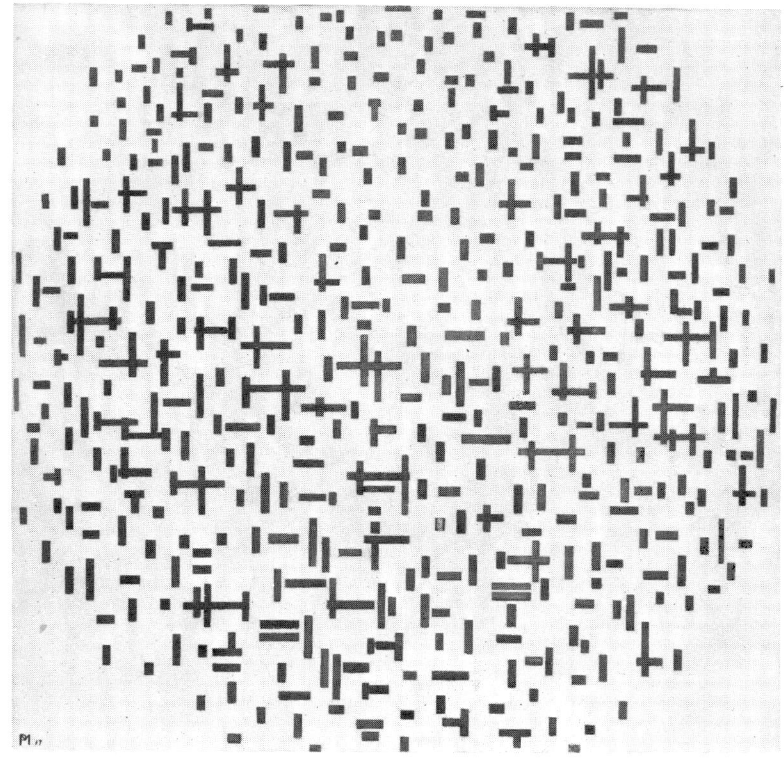

78 *Composition with Lines* 1917

LAREN

In summer, from 1915 onwards, Mondrian often worked at Laren, a village not far from Amsterdam frequented by a good many artists. He first lodged with the composer Jakob van Domselaer, with whom he had made friends in Paris in 1912, then, later, he moved into a small studio of his own. While he was at Laren, he made the acquaintance of Salomon B. Slijper, who regularly spent his vacations at nearby Blaricum. Slijper soon became his friend, confidant and

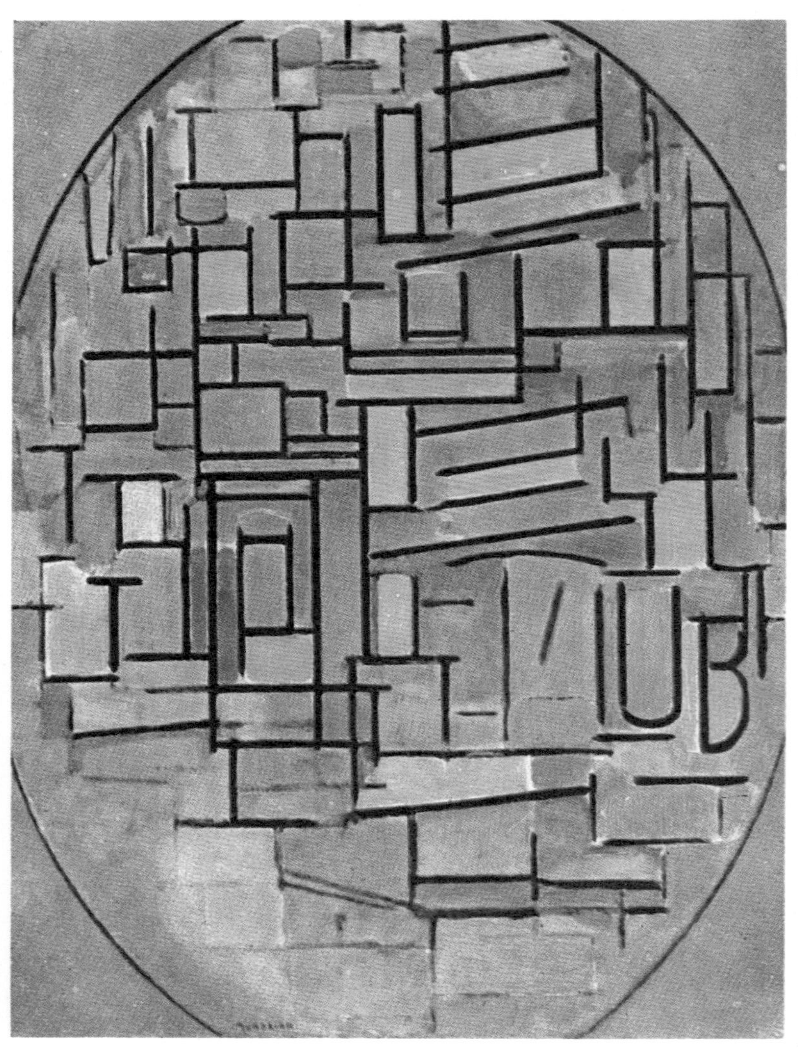

79 *Oval Composition* 1913–14

patron and took such a keen interest in Mondrian's work that he managed to collect, in the next few years, nearly two hundred of his pictures and drawings, mostly those produced between 1908 and 1914. This was the period he preferred,

80 *Composition* 1916

and, thanks to his collection, now on loan exhibition at the Gemeentemuseum at The Hague, it is possible for us to get a very complete idea of the transition period during which Mondrian gradually freed himself from naturalism and was converted to abstraction.

Salomon B. Slijper's interest was seconded by the art critic H.P. Bremner who, as adviser to Mrs H. Kröller-Müller, formed the collection which has since become a national museum. Bremner's interest lasted, unfortunately, at most for two or three years, for, in 1919, he renounced the financial agreement he had made with Mondrian, to whom it had been of considerable help. With one exception, in 1923, Bremner did not buy one of his works after 1920. The critic's favour had turned elsewhere, to the benefit of another artist, Bart van der Leck.

VAN DER LECK

Van der Leck was not unknown to Mondrian. They had met in 1916 at The Hague. They met again in Blaricum where they worked in close association. A former pupil of Professor Derkinderen, held in high esteem by the younger generation of Dutch artists, influenced by Breitner, Toulouse-Lautrec and Van Gogh, Bart van der Leck expressed in his figures a strange blend of sarcasm, irony and pity. In 1914 his style had changed. He abandoned perspective, modelling, modulations of values, and began to apply his colours flat and to outline his forms with hard contours. Under Mondrian's influence he made a clean break with illusionist realism in favour of geometrical stylization and, ultimately, of abstraction. Van der Leck was a painter of undeniable talent, of great possibilities and promise, which he unfortunately squandered by his excessive dogmatism and his boundless self-esteem.

There is no doubt, however, that Mondrian was, in his turn, influenced by Van der Leck. 'Van der Leck,' he wrote, 'though still figurative, painted in compact planes of pure colour. My more or less cubist technique – in consequence

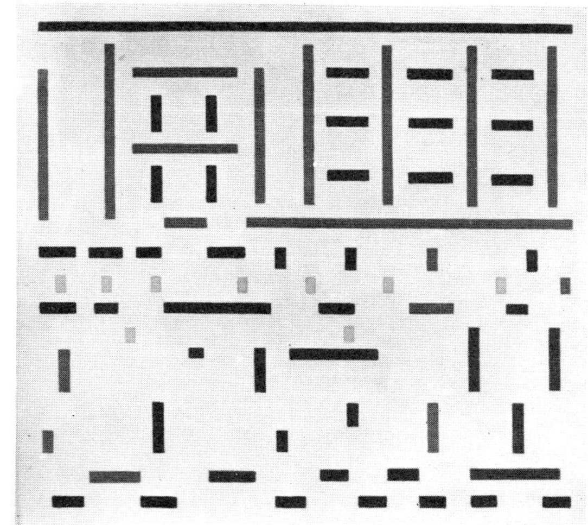

81
Bart van der Leck
Geometric Composition No. 1 1917

82
Bart van der Leck
Geometric Composition No. 2 1917

still more or less pictorial – underwent the influence of his exact technique.'

Indeed, from this time on, Mondrian abandoned networks of lines and broken colours, and, without any kind of transition, began to paint, on surfaces as neutral as possible, squares and rectangles in clear, flat colours harmoniously spaced, as
Ill. 86 in his *Composition with Colour Planes on White Ground A*

83 *Composition in Blue B* 1917

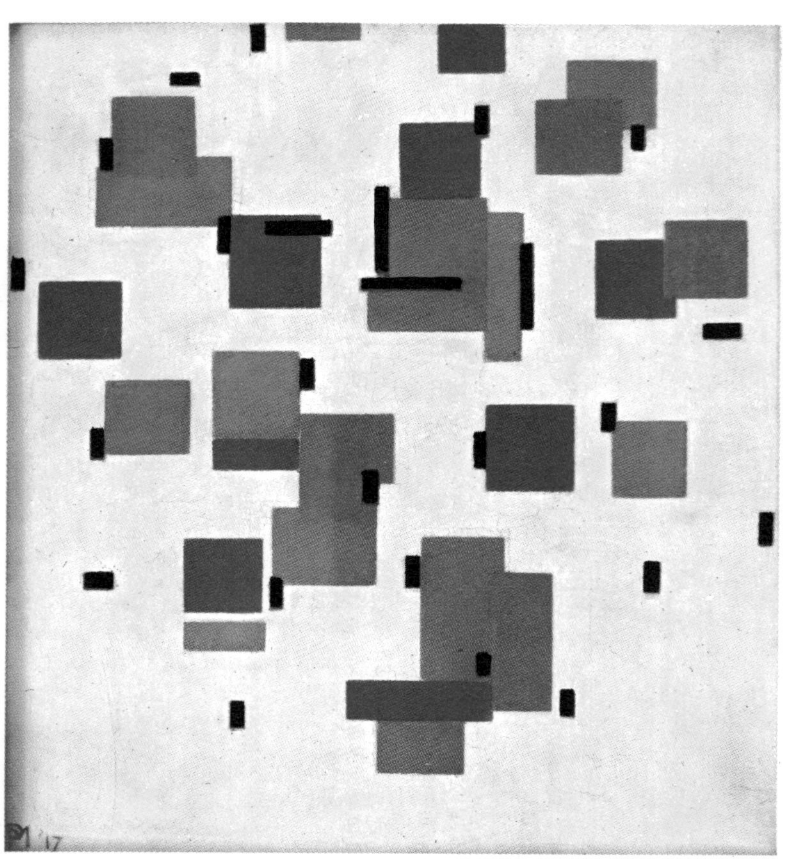

84 *Composition No. 3 with Colour Planes* 1917

(1917), now in the Kröller-Müller Museum at Otterlo. The same year he produced another six compositions in the same style, before returning to a less diffuse, more concentrated manner. One thing is quite certain: the naturalist works of the two painters do not bear comparison. Van der Leck's are, from every point of view, superior to Mondrian's. But the name of Van der Leck will probably be forgotten when Mondrian's is still receiving the homage due to one of those great creative artists of the twentieth century who transformed western painting in its structures, its directions and its objectives.

At Laren, Mondrian also made the acquaintance of M.H.J. Schoenmaekers, a former Catholic priest and the author of popular works on philosophy, with whom he immediately discovered affinities of thought. In spite of his vague mysticism, Schoenmaekers wrote most intelligibly. Some of his books, particularly his *New Image of the World (Het nieuwe Wereldbeeld),* found in Mondrian a reader predisposed to accept their message. He certainly adopted a part of the philosopher's doctrine and terminology, although Schoenmaekers' intelligence and too brilliant conversation induced in him a certain mistrust, for Mondrian knew himself to be far less well-endowed with wit and eloquence. Nevertheless, it is possible to detect in Mondrian's writings after this time certain remarks and expressions obviously borrowed from the works of Schoenmaekers.

85
Composition with Colour Planes B
1917

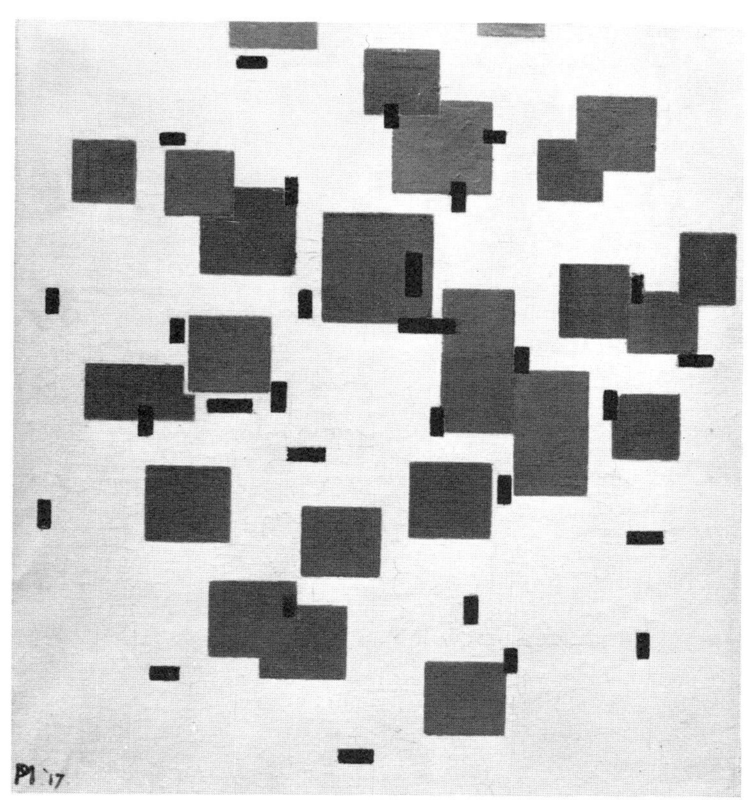

86
Composition with Colour Planes on White Ground A
1917

Personally inclined to meditation, deeply concerned with matters of religion and always actively interested in theosophy, Mondrian liked to exchange ideas with the author of the *New Image of the World*. This interest in theosophy was probably engendered by books which he had come upon by chance twenty years previously, during one of the religious upheavals caused by his Calvinist upbringing. That is certainly, according to Albert van den Briel, how Édouard Schuré's book *Les Grands Initiés* had come to make a great impression on him. We know, too, that in 1909 Mondrian had joined the Theosophical Society of Holland.

87 *Composition. Colour Planes with Grey Contours* 1918

He read works by Mme Blavatsky, Annie Besant and Krishnamurti, representing the Oriental tradition of the theosophical movement, as well as the writings of the anthroposophist Rudolf Steiner, the champion of Christian esotericism. Literature of this kind was a determining factor in Mondrian's intellectual development. As Martin James wrote *(Art News* 1957): 'Mondrian's theosophy was more than a personal quirk. Several artists around 1910 sought through it deeper and more universal values, meaning behind meaning, new dimensions to understanding. The thought that the ancient seers perceived and imparted a veiled wisdom, that behind the many guises of truth there is *one* truth, is partly based on Oriental and Neo-Platonic ideas; it easily links with the romantic and symbolist theory of illuminism, which gives the artist extraordinary, even occult power of insight into the nature of the world, the reality behind appearances – a new content for art.'

Mondrian was far too discreet, far too modest to display his mystical speculations, too reserved to make any attempt to share them and too respectful of other people's privacy to set out to make proselytes.

In 1909 he was a member of the Theosophical Society of Holland and, though he later withdrew his membership, he remained a faithful supporter. In Paris, he used to keep in his cupboard, along with the numbers of *De Stijl* to which he had contributed and a few copies of his essay *Le Néo-Plasticisme,* published by Léonce Rosenberg in 1920, a copy of *Het nieuwe Wereldbeeld* by Schoenmaekers. That constituted his entire library, for he never accumulated books, probably because he was afraid they would encumber not only his studio but his way of thinking, and divert it from its total concentration on the aim he had set himself.

Why Mondrian withdrew from the Theosophical Society no one has been able to discover. Nevertheless, even when his faith in neo-plasticism had supplanted his theosophical preoccupations, he never totally abandoned metaphysical thought. Nor did he ever forget his exchanges with the philosopher of Laren nor the ideas embodied in *Het nieuwe Wereldbeeld.* It was with the title of that book in mind that he came to give his own theory the name neo-plasticism *(nieuwe Beelding).* But this was only part of his debt to the Dutch theosophist.

Perhaps even more fruitful in its consequences was Mondrian's association with Theo van Doesburg, painter, interior decorator, writer and lecturer. It led to the creation, in 1917, of the *avant-garde* review *De Stijl*. The two artists had met as the result of a particularly eulogistic reference to Mondrian in an article Van Doesburg had written, for a paper of very limited circulation, on an exhibition at the Stedelijk Museum, Amsterdam, which brought together works by Mondrian, Sluyters, Gestel, Van Epen and the French artist Le Fauconnier. From then on, they worked in close association. Mondrian was forty-three and Van Doesburg only thirty-two. It is typical of both that, whereas Mondrian modified his family name by simply dropping one of its two a's, Van Doesburg discarded his altogether. His real name was Charles E. M. Küpper.

The two men could not have been more divergent in character. Mondrian was reflective, circumspect, obstinate, self-contained; Van Doesburg was impulsive, versatile, quick to enthuse and quick to dislike. The painter Jean Hélion, who knew him well, describes Van Doesburg as 'cordial and at the same time vulnerable; he would fly into a rage with a great display of emotion. He loved to throw stones into the pool and fling his articles in the public's face. He had no difficulty in asserting the contrary of what he had said the day before. He contradicted everybody with obvious prejudice, and defended anyone who was the subject of attack. He argued with the fauves, the surrealists and the cubists as much as with his own neo-plasticists, and with him every discussion was always a battle.'

One has only to confront the two founders of *De Stijl* to be immediately aware of their different intellectual status. In the case of Van Doesburg, it was impatience, feverish action and the taste for polemics and proselytizing, combined with ambition, which urged him to prospect for new means of expression. In Mondrian's, it was the slow deliberation, the extreme patience of the artist looking in secret for indefinable perfection and hating to impose it or make it a source of personal triumph. Mondrian was a kind of clear-sighted *illuminé* to whom the certitude of faith is sufficient. Van Doesburg was the painter-critic; Mondrian the thinker and the poet.

Because each complemented the other, they were able to harness themselves to the same task, and maintain for a period of seven years the coherence of the movement they had created. Van Doesburg unquestionably provided the energy and Mondrian the conscience. But it had needed all young Van Doesburg's persuasive insistence and over twelve months of discussions to succeed in overcoming the natural reticence of the elder collaborator.

88
Theo van Doesburg
Contre Composition
1924

CHAPTER FOUR

Neo-plasticism

The art review *De Stijl* first appeared in October 1917. Contributors to the first issue were Van der Leck, the Hungarian painter Vilmos Huszar, the Belgian painter and sculptor Georges Vantongerloo, the poet Antonie Kok, the architects J.J.P. Oud, Jan Wils and Robert van't Hoff, the Italian futurist Gino Severini and, naturally, Theo van Doesburg and Piet Mondrian.

Ill. 89

Van der Leck soon broke away from the group, but other artists joined it, including the architects Rietveld (in 1919) and Van Eesteren (in 1923), and the painters Vordemberge-Gildewart, Cesar Domela and Kiesler. Actually, there was never any concerted movement as such. Most of those who wrote for the review did not know one another. Van Doesburg even thought it preferable for them not to meet, though he carefully fostered among his collaborators and correspondents a common line of thought which did not fail to have fruitful results.

DE STIJL

The manifestos printed in the early issues of *De Stijl* were inspired by Mondrian and Van Doesburg. Here are some of its postulates: 'To build up a spiritual community among artists and to foster the creation of a collective style; to bring about the integration of arts and techniques, particularly in architecture. The plastic must derive not from exterior

89
Vilmos Huszar
Composition
1916

vision but from interior life, not from imitation but from representation; the new spirit is the enemy of animal spontaneity (lyricism); painting must be made to submit to the horizontal-vertical order, which excludes the diagonal and the curve; colours must be limited to the three primary colours and the three non-colours white, black and grey, which must never be either mixed or superimposed (cookery).'

The aesthetic and spiritual objectives of *De Stijl* were defined as follows:

'What we want is a new aesthetic based on pure relationships of lines and pure colours, because only pure relationships between pure constructive elements can result in pure beauty. At the present time not only is pure beauty necessary to us, but it is, in our estimation, the only means capable of a pure manifestation of the universal force which is to be found

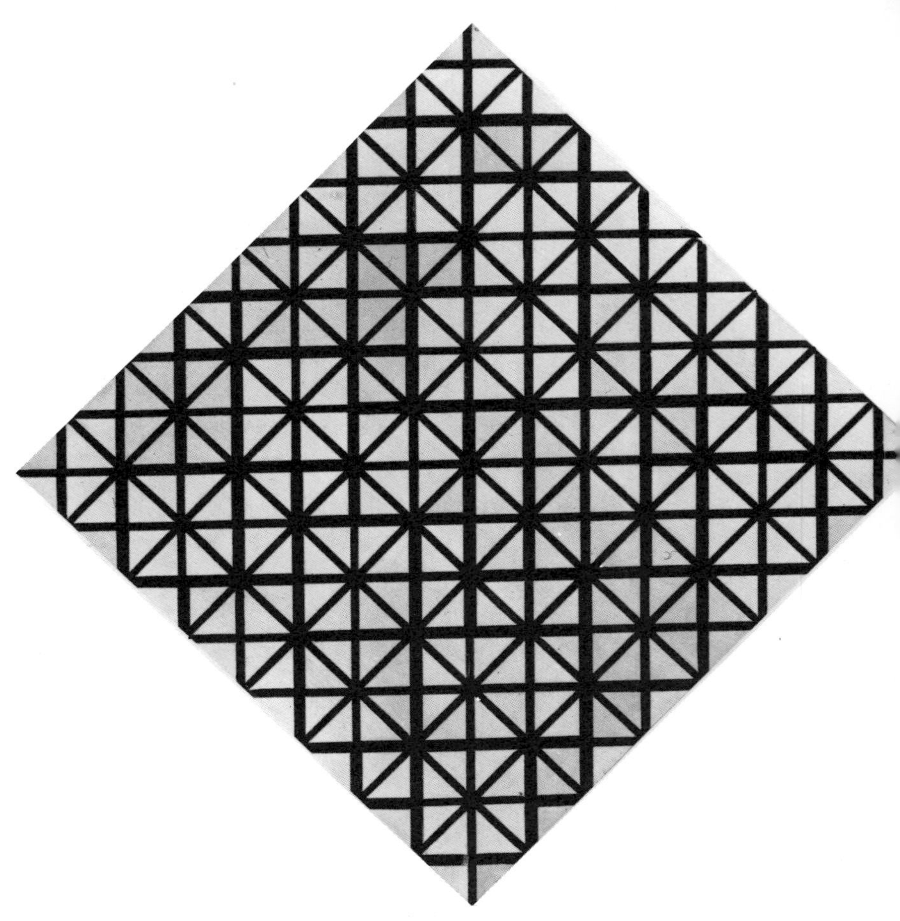

90 *Composition. Lozenge with Grey Lines* 1918

in all things. It is identical with what was revealed in the past under the name of Divinity and which is indispensable to the poor human beings we are if we are to live and achieve an equilibrium, for things in themselves are opposed to us and matter in its most exterior form is armed against us.'

These principles became, with time, less dogmatic. Mondrian alone remained steadfastly faithful to them. However, the outstanding merit of *De Stijl* was that it launched ideas

91 *Lozenge Composition* 1919

which were new and extremely original for their time, not only in Holland but in Europe generally. These ideas, one is forced to admit, were not always very clearly expressed. But although their formulation was often laborious and even clumsy, it revealed, at least in the case of Mondrian, a man who was not only accustomed to thinking deeply about his art but, what is more, was capable of speculations of a much broader nature. In the following extract from the article he contributed to the first number of *De Stijl,* we discover the extent of his involvement:

'The life of modern cultured man is gradually turning away from natural things and becoming more and more abstract.

'With natural (exterior) things becoming more and more automatic, we find our vital attention concentrating more and more on internal things. The life of truly modern man is neither purely material nor purely emotional; it manifests itself rather as a more autonomous life of the increasingly self-conscious mind.

'This also applies to art. Art is on the way to becoming the product of another duality in man: the product of a cultivated exteriority and a more conscious, a more profound inner awareness. As pure representation of the human mind art will go on to express itself in a purified, that is an abstract form.

'The truly modern artist is consciously aware of the abstraction in an emotion of beauty; he consciously acknowledges that the emotion aroused by beauty is cosmic, is universal. This conscious acknowledgement leads to an abstract plastic expression, limited only to what is universal.

'Neo-plasticism cannot assume the form of a natural or concrete representation which, it is true, always indicates to a certain extent, the universal, or at least carries it hidden within itself. Neither could it take on the appearance of things which characterize the particular, that is, natural form and natural colour. It must, on the contrary, find its expression in the abstraction of all form and colour, that is, in the straight line and in clearly defined primary colour.'

That article was only the first of many. In 1919 and 1920 Mondrian published, also in *De Stijl,* under the title *Natural Reality and Abstract Reality,* eleven articles written as a series of Platonic dialogues between a layman, a naturalist painter and an 'abstract-realist' painter. These dialogues, together

92
Composition in Grey and Light Brown
1918

with Kandinsky's memorable work *On the Spiritual in Art*, published as early as 1911, constitute the basic texts of modern abstract art. (The authors of these two pivotal works, while starting from identical bases and even making similar initial moves, were to pursue their goal in markedly different ways.) Although Mondrian illustrated his doctrine in pictures which became more austere and refined, he also was to develop it in some thirty articles and publications. We shall discuss only two of the most important ones, the pamphlet

Le Néo-Plasticisme, published in 1920 by L'Effort Moderne, and the collection of essays in English, *Plastic Art and Pure Plastic Art,* published by Wittenborn in New York the year after his death (1945).

'FATHER OF NEO-PLASTICISM'

De Stijl was the vehicle for an aesthetic based on geometrical abstraction of which Mondrian, with an inflexible will, had made himself the prophet. Before neo-plasticism itself was propagated in Holland, he had started a movement for the renewal of aesthetic ideals which was to affect not only painting but architecture and the decorative and graphic arts generally. Van der Leck's claims to the paternity of the new doctrine are not altogether justified. Of course the history of art is full of disputes of this kind: one need only recall the quarrel between Émile Bernard and Gauguin which still sets critics at loggerheads. If, as he claimed, Émile Bernard *did* discover cloisonnism, it was certainly Gauguin who expounded it, and simultaneously practised it with sovereign authority. In almost the same way, Mondrian was the unquestioned master of neo-plasticism. As early as 1922, Van Doesburg, in his editorial of the fifth anniversary number of *De Stijl,* expressed without the slightest qualification the homage due to Mondrian on this point. Van Doesburg, in fact, sees the origins of the movement in the pictures Mondrian painted in 1913, or thereabouts, and concludes by hailing him as 'the father of neo-plasticism'.

Two years after this accolade, however, Mondrian withdrew his collaboration with *De Stijl*, reproaching Van Doesburg for having betrayed the ideals for which they had both campaigned. Van Doesburg, an excitable, unstable person, always in quest of novelty, had first flirted with

93
Composition
1919

94 Theo van Doesburg. Décor for Café Aubette, Strasbourg 1926–7

dadaism in 1922, and then, in 1924, launched his own manifesto on behalf of elementarism, in which he renounced the
Ill. 88 dogma of the 'horizontal-vertical' in favour of the diagonal. He was given the opportunity to apply his new aesthetic in 1928, in the decoration of a restaurant in Strasbourg,
Ill. 94 L'Aubette, now remodelled. Van Doesburg thought that Mondrian was simply marking time; Mondrian had come to the conclusion that Van Doesburg was a dangerous troublemaker. The break was inevitable. When it came, Mondrian was left to stand alone in defence of his credo.

To discover the primary reason for neo-plasticism we must look at the character, the temperament, the idiosyncratic nature of Mondrian himself. From his childhood dominated by the harsh, sententious authority of his father, from his Calvinist upbringing and his own religious inclinations, Mondrian had inherited an austere philosophy of life. His original faith was diverted towards theosophy and his interest in theosophy was eventually absorbed by the aesthetic he discovered, and which he defended staunchly to his dying day. Throughout, he remained a man of high moral conscience compelled to exercise unceasing self-control, and aspiring at all times to transcendent, unalterable objectivity.

There was something of the preacher in him, a quality emphasized by his physical appearance. His dress was always scrupulously correct, always meticulously neat, even though his garments were threadbare. His demeanour was that of a rather buttoned-up *petit bourgeois*, his features those of any run-of-the-mill office-worker; these, combined with the reticence that pervaded his entire personality, made him appear insignificant. Solitary, retiring, taciturn, he could be courteous and kindly in his relations with others. He never paraded his disdain for wealth, honours and titles, perhaps fearing that his native pride might be mistaken for

95 *Self-portrait* c. 1918

arrogance. Nothing in either his appearance or his talk revealed the privations inherent in his poverty.

One of his friends, Antoine Pevsner, used to tell an amusing story about Mondrian's hard life. When he was living in Paris, Mondrian's budding reputation attracted the suspicions of the tax-collector for the fourteenth *arrondissement*, who paid a surprise visit to the Rue du Départ, in the hope of

96 *Composition with Red, Blue, Black and Yellow-Green* 1920

discovering 'obvious signs of wealth' in the studio of this defaulting tax-payer. He found Mondrian busy preparing his inevitable soup. Faced with the monastic starkness of the studio and the revolting brew simmering on the gas-ring, the disconcerted tax-man withdrew without further investigation.

Michel Seuphor has described Mondrian as a rather crotchety old bachelor who did all his own housework, shopping, cooking – and even darning. Indeed, one or two unfortunate romantic ventures had turned him against marriage, for which he was, in any case, unsuited.

This man, who wrote almost as much as he painted, who

97 *Composition in Grey, Red, Yellow and Blue* 1920

invented an aesthetic doctrine which laid the foundations of an intellectual art, was, paradoxically, not a great intellectual himself. He was neither particularly well-informed nor notably cultured. But, since he had a taste for theoretical ideas, and was naturally inclined to speculative thought, he was able to set out in search of a dogma as imperative as the Ten Commandments. The elements of this dogma he drew from the religious austerity of his childhood and, later, from the metaphysics of Schoenmaekers, whose theories of 'positive mysticism' and 'plastic mathematics' exerted on the mind of his pupil an influence which should not be underestimated.

'The expression *plastic mathematics*', Schoenmaekers explained, 'signifies true and methodical thought on the part of the creator . . . Only now are we learning to translate reality in our imagination by constructions controllable by reason in such a way as to recover these same constructions eventually in the concrete attributes of nature, thus achieving a penetration of nature by means of plastic vision.'

It is not difficult to imagine such words coming from one of Mondrian's own numerous writings. In his monograph on *De Stijl* H. L. C. Jaffé, to show how much the artist owed to the philosopher, has compared passages from works by Schoenmaekers and Mondrian, making it clear that Mondrian found in the conversation and the writings of his mentor the wherewithal to justify his own inclination towards abstrac-

98 *Composition. Checkerboard, Dark Colours* 1919

99 *Composition. Checkerboard, Bright Colours* 1919

tion in art. When Schoenmaekers said: 'Our desire is to penetrate nature in such a way as to reveal the internal structure of the real', it was no more than a translation of Mondrian's intentions as he was to express them later in his own unpolished, gritty phraseology.

It was also Schoenmaekers who said: 'However persistent, however capricious it may be in its variations, nature always functions fundamentally with absolute regularity, that is, with plastic regularity.' It is a sentence which reads like the very source of neo-plasticism. Mondrian himself said that painting offers the artist a means as exact as mathematics of interpreting the essential facts of nature.

Just as his relations with Van der Leck modified the style of his work, it would appear that, at one decisive moment in Mondrian's career, the ideas of Schoenmaekers so ordered the evolution of his thought that neo-plasticism assumed that exaggeratedly conceptual aspect for which it is still criticized. Mondrian was clearly not a sensualist, but he was nonetheless very sensitive, too timid, too reserved to indulge in emotional outbursts. He felt nothing but repugnance for the flashy trappings of romanticism, the unbridled display of feelings,

100 *Composition* 1921

101
Composition with Red, Yellow and Blue 1921

the long intense interludes, the brilliant improvisations and the hasty workmanship.

Like Robespierre, who denounced 'the abasement of the human self', Mondrian loathed sentimentality and effusive emotionalism. 'I hate', he said, 'everything approaching temperamental inspiration, "sacred fire" and all those attributes of genius which serve only as cloaks for untidy minds.' We must not be surprised, therefore, to find that the distinctive elements of neo-plasticism are its objectivity, its anti-individualism, its pretensions to the permanent and the universal, its needs for total perfection. 'Austerity, lucidity, impassivity' is the motto the artist ought to have inscribed over the door of his studio.

102 *Composition. Bright Colour Planes with Grey Lines* 1919

Mondrian's early works, particularly those painted between 1908 and 1911, with their broad, rapid brushstrokes saturated with strong colours, might give one the impression that his art was destined, like that of so many Dutch artists,
Ill. 32 to be slack and expressionistic. The *Red Tree*, the *Lighthouse*

at Westkapelle, the *Windmill in Sunlight* each reveal a tendency towards the most impetuous lyricism. But, as we have seen, this tendency was suddenly and firmly repressed by the revelation of cubism. It was cubism that set Mondrian on the only road consistent with his genius. It may seem out of place to use a word that is so recklessly bandied about to describe a man whose work is the result of such a long and patient quest. Yet this artist, who worked so slowly, with stubborn obstinacy and cold-blooded frenzy, who was determined to *Ills 27–8*

103 *Composition. Bright Colour Planes with Grey Lines* 1919

climb one by one the steps which separated his effort from his goal, discovered a theory so completely new and original, so simple, so limpid, so obvious that it almost defies analysis. It is a theory founded on horizontal-vertical dualism, on the right-angle, on the exclusive use of the three primary colours and the three 'non-colours', black, white and grey. That is all neo-plasticism is. But it is just there that, according to Mondrian, the immutable truth lies. With it, he undertook to visually reconstruct the world.

THE LAWS OF NEO-PLASTICISM

Mondrian summed up his theory in these words:

'Denaturalization being one of the essential points of human progress, it is of the greatest importance in neo-plastic art. It is the privilege of neo-plastic painting to have demonstrated plastically the necessity for denaturalization. It has denaturalized both constructive elements and the manner of composing them. That is why it is genuine abstract painting. To denaturalize is to abstract. By abstraction one attains purely abstract expression.'

According to Mondrian, then, the modern painter must turn completely away from nature and seek inspiration in his own mind. He must cease to offer an image of the exterior world or the illusion of sensory reality; he must substitute a new, autonomous reality which is valid both in itself and by itself. To discover external, universal, absolute truth and essential reality, as opposed to the contingent, fallacious truth of nature, was Mondrian's ambition.

'Why', he wrote in 1920, in his *Natural Reality and Abstract Reality*, 'should universal beauty continue to appear in art under a veiled or covert form, while in the sciences, for instance, the trend is toward the greatest possible clarity? Why should art continue to follow nature when every other

104 *Composition with Large Blue Plane and Red and Yellow Rectangles* 1921

field has left nature behind? Why does not art manifest itself as non-natural or "other" in relation to nature?'

It is surprising that, in his search for pure beauty, an artist born in a country where aesthetic tradition was always based on the attentive observation and the most detailed reproduction of nature, that a descendant of Vermeer, Ruysdael,

105 *Composition with Red, Blue and Yellow-Green* 1920

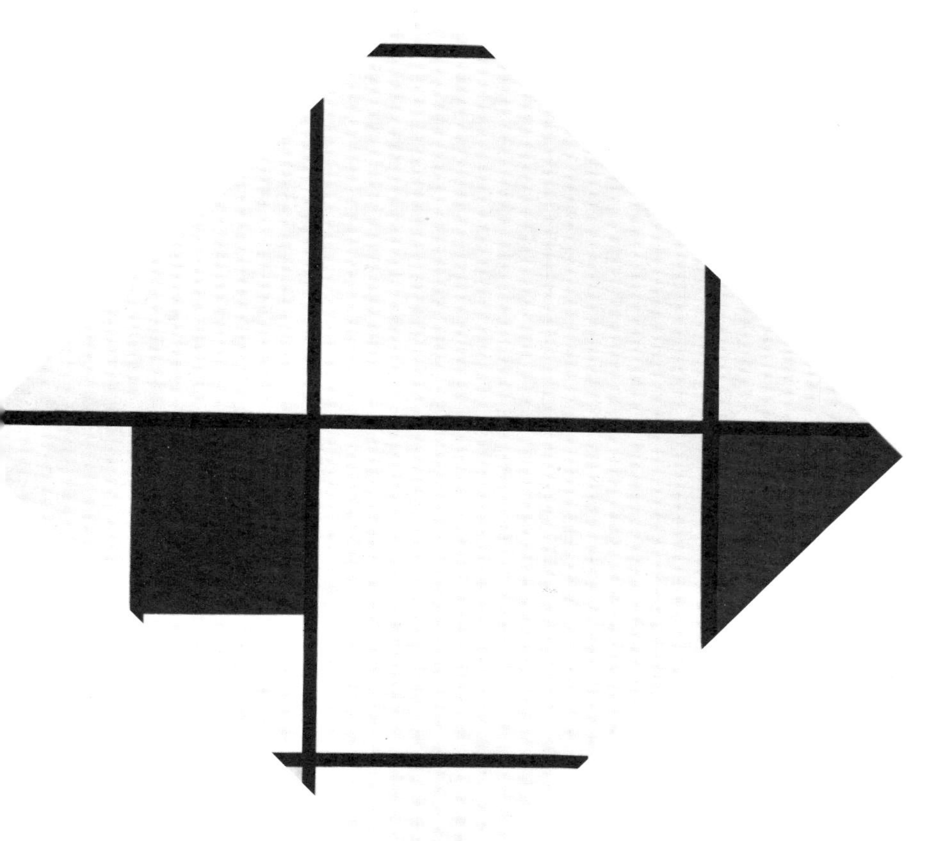

106 *Composition in a Square* 1921

Van Ostade, Van de Velde and all the portrait- and landscape-painters whose chief ambition was the scrupulous presentation of the people and things of their own country, their own times, families and friends, should have been the first to condemn outright, and with so much authority and energy, the circumscribed naturalism of traditional copyists and to advocate a style so completely stripped of all contingencie that, from the outset, it was raised to the inviolate summit of abstraction.

Once he had defined his doctrine, Mondrian drew up a list of general principles in an essay he wrote in French, with the assistance of Michel Seuphor. Though written in 1926, this essay was not published until 1949, under the title *Le Home, la Rue, la Cité*. In it he states the following six principles:

'(1) The plastic medium should be the flat plane or the rectangular prism in primary colours (red, blue and yellow) and in non-colour (white, black and grey). In architecture, empty space counts as non-colour. The material can count as colour.

'(2) There must be an equivalence of plastic means. Different in size and colour, they should nevertheless have equal value. In general, equilibrium implies a large uncoloured surface or an empty space, and a rather small surface of colour or matter.

'(3) The duality of opposing elements in the plastic medium is also required in the composition.

'(4) Constant equilibrium is achieved through opposition and is expressed by the straight line (limit of the plastic means) in its principal apposition, i.e., the right-angle.

'(5) The equilibrium that neutralizes and annihilates the plastic means is achieved through the proportions within which those means are placed, and which create the living rhythm.

'(6) All symmetry must be excluded.'

One can see in this scheme, on the extreme conciseness, of which Mondrian insisted, traces of that abrupt dogmatism which so irritated his detractors, who interpreted its intellectual passion for the absolute as inhuman frigidity. And yet, in spite of his apparently inhuman attitude, beneath his intransigent doctrinaire exterior, Mondrian was a sensitive, contemplative man, capable of scaling the heights of poetry.

POETRY

To be convinced of this one need only read a few pages of the series of dialogues entitled *Natural Reality and Abstract Reality*. In one of these, the three characters are shown walking, just after nightfall, on a sandy plain beneath a starlit sky. The silence and the majesty of the night inspire the three friends to discuss human pettiness. Contemplation, they decide, is indispensable to man, if he is to overcome his precarious condition, and to the artist if he is to perceive the image

:07 *Tableau No. I* 1921–5

of perfect harmony, of supreme equilibrium, of permanent and eternal beauty.

In the gradual exposition of his ideas Mondrian's emotion grows stronger and his poetic feeling more exalted. Individual sensitivity, he says, must efface itself before universal sensitivity, which can be expressed in an adequate manner only by

108 *Composition* 1921

109 *Composition with Red, Yellow and Blue* 1921

pure, abstract plasticity. And this is, in most cases, either hidden or disturbed by the contingencies of nature or material harassments of the individual. He concludes: 'Truth is the principle of the new age, just as love was that of the previous age. Then, it was love that veiled; now love itself is veiled . . . in truth. Love, in growing, has become truth.'

If, in the course of his poetic experience, Mondrian wished

110 *Composition* 1922

for 'a new meaning and a new expressive value for words', does that mean it is possible to speak, as the Italian critic Filiberto Menna does in his book on Mondrian published in 1962, of affinities with post-Baudelairian French poetry, and, in particular, with Mallarmé? I do not think so. Mondrian's thought ran in a closed circuit. In his exceptionally inspired writings, such as those we have just mentioned, there is nothing which could possibly allow us to share Filiberto Menna's contention. It is well known that Mondrian had an instinctive distrust of anything approaching literature, and especially of anything 'literary' in a work of art.

111 *Composition c.* 1922

112
Composition in a Square with Red, Yellow and Blue c. 1925

THE AVANT-GARDE

Like other great creators who are aware that their powers, however vast, will barely be sufficient to complete their chosen task, Mondrian showed only aversion and indifference to anything that caused him to deviate in the slightest degree from the path he had chosen to follow. When Van Doesburg succumbed to the attractions of futurism and

113 *Composition with Red, Yellow, Blue and Black* 1921

dadaism, Mondrian's reaction to these *avant-garde* movements bordered on repulsion. He was greatly concerned when in 1920 (he was in Paris at the time) he read Van Doesburg's pronouncement in *De Stijl*: 'if, behind *non-sense* is hidden a meaning more profound than the rule itself, then *non-sense* is not only permissible, but actually necessary. On these lines dadaism intends to create new super-sensual rules.'

In his essay *Neo-Plasticism,* published in 1920, Mondrian condemned futurism in these words: 'The futurists wished to liberate the word from the idea. D. Braga says: "Henceforth art will dispense with the idea. It is the idea which serves as a vehicle for the past . . . Marinetti hates intelligence." Is it possible to discount intelligence in modern man, if he is affected by aesthetic emotion? For the new man feeling and intelligence are one. When he thinks, he feels, when he feels, he thinks . . . If the futurists hate intelligence, it is because they still think, on this particular question, along the lines of the old mentality.'

When, as he occasionally does, he concedes a point, he immediately withdraws it: 'Neo-plasticism', he writes, 'agrees with the futurists in desiring to eliminate the *self* from art. But it goes even further. For one sees, from the art of the futurists, that they do not know the consequences of the new plasticism. They wanted to replace the already exhausted "psychology of man" by "the lyrical obsession of matter". Futurism appeals, above all, to sensation. It is the frenzification of ambience.'

He also makes another, quite unexpected concession when he says: 'In a futurist manifesto the proclamation of hatred of woman (the feminine) is entirely justified. It is the Woman in Man that is the direct cause of the dominance of the tragic in art.' By 'tragic' he means impulse, romanticism, sentimentality, mannerism, baroque, everything, in short, that he detested.

It is understandable that a man so completely imbued with order and purity, so grimly intent upon the expression of the universal and the timeless, should have found it impossible

114 *Tableau No. II* 1921–5

to react otherwise than with the utmost severity to the subversive will to destroy proclaimed by the dadaists. 'A few advanced spirits', he wrote, 'reject logic completely. Is that the way to liberate art? Is not art the very exteriorization of

115 *Composition with Red, Yellow and Blue* 1921

116 *Tableau I* 1921

logic? One can no more liberate word from thought by setting down words one after the other, as the dadaists wished to do, than one can prevent there being some kind of connecting link between them.'

In the same essay we also find him already in revolt against the anti-intellectual attitude the surrealists were later to

117
Composition in White and Black 1926

118
Composition I with Blue and Yellow 1925

assume. He writes: 'The unconscious in us warns us that in art we have to follow one particular path. And if we follow it, it is not the sign of an unconscious act. On the contrary, it shows that there is in our ordinary consciousness a greater awareness of our unconsciousness.'

At a time when artistic circles, torn between expressionism, traditional realism and dadaism, were in such a state of

119 *Composition* 1921

ferment, Mondrian was advancing unperturbed along the road opened to him by cubism and leading towards the intellectualization of art: objective beauty and pure abstraction.

CHAPTER FIVE

Between the wars

The war over, Mondrian returned to Paris, probably in February 1919, though, according to the Laren municipal records, it was in July. This time he did not go to the French capital to seek inspiration; he arrived there fully armed with his own doctrine. The time had come when he had no further need for reference and example, and when he considered himself in a strong enough position to offer his own art as an example and, if need be, to impose it. For the thirty remaining years of his life he exploited dispassionately and without concessions the same system.

The year before he left Holland, Mondrian had painted a composition set in a 'lozenge' in which a grid of vertical and horizontal parallels cutting each other at regular intervals produced an even number of small lozenges *(Composition: Lozenge with Grey Lines,* Gemeentemuseum, The Hague). *Ill. 90*
As he built up this series of square patterns, he introduced, at a very early stage, contrasts of opaque and grey lines, the idea being to diminish their ornamental appearance. But he was still not satisfied and, as soon as he was back in Paris, he took up the same theme once more, this time dividing the lozenge into squares and rectangles of different sizes, all in bright colours *(Composition: Bright Colour Planes with Grey Lines,* *Ill. 102*
Kröller-Müller Museum, Otterlo). He also painted, in 1919, compositions in checkerboard form, perfectly regular in their divisions, but with a subtle animation produced by the alternation of light and dark squares.

At the end of 1919 and in 1920, the geometrical planes resulting from the crossing of verticals and horizontals increase in size and diminish in number, while their asymmetry becomes more marked. Gradually the lines thicken, composition is clarified, colour is more sustained and one of the planes is separated from the rest and covers the greater part of the surface. Determined to simplify further, and to reduce and condense his means of expression, Mondrian finally succeeded, by sheer perseverance, in attaining the greatest intensity in utter starkness.

By 1921 he had at last discovered the method and the language exactly suited to his thought. His straight lines are

120
Composition III with Red, Yellow and Blue 1927

121 *Composition in a Square* 1926

now so thick that they too look like planes. The canvas is almost entirely occupied by one single rectangle or one single square. While they are being used more and more sparingly, the three primary colours gain in density and brightness
(Composition with Large Blue Plane and Red and Yellow *Ill. 104*
Rectangles, Sydney Janis Gallery, New York; *Composition*
with Red, Yellow, Blue and Black, Gemeentemuseum, The *Ill. 113*
Hague).

Mondrian's work of the next few years may give the impression that he simply repeated himself. But, on closer observation, his compositions, while becoming markedly more restrained, prove to be singularly different from each

122
Composition with Red, Yellow and Blue 1927

other and diversified in the size, colouring and arrangements of the quadrilateral planes, the whole work being thought out, prepared and executed with the patience and attention to detail of the true ascetic. Mondrian is now without question master of his medium. His search has finally led him to a style so coherent and so balanced that it would be impossible to

123 *Fox Trot A* 1927

eliminate anything from his pictures without destroying their structure. Here, a millimetre too little or too much, a duller red, a less intense blue; there, a side of a rectangle slightly shorter, an intersection of straight lines nearer to or farther from the edge of the canvas, and the entire work would begin to totter like badly-seated scaffolding.

Mondrian's art is not to be written off as the impoverished expression of a man of limited outlook, wrapped up in his own dialectic. There is much more in it than discipline, reasoning and logic; there is finesse and subtlety, and ingenuity. The red square (actually, Mondrian's 'squares' are rarely perfect equilaterals) which spreads its immensity over the picture in the Bartos Collection in New York *(Composition with Red, Blue and Yellow,* 1930) may, in other cases, be reduced to a slim band and be pushed away into a corner of the
Ill. 125 canvas *(Composition with Red, Yellow and Blue,* 1927, Sidney Janis Gallery, New York). Though generally square, his

124
Composition with Red, Yellow and Blue 1928

125
Composition with Red, Yellow and Blue 1927

format may also be rectangular or rhomboid. In 1921 and 1922 he used all three primary colours; later he used only two, or even only one. In the period of his *Compositions with Black Lines* (1930–3) he stopped using colour altogether. This period marks the zenith of his achievement. Colour now adds nothing, in fact, to the significance of the picture. The scarcer his coloured surfaces become the more convincing is the finished work. When the whiteness of the canvas is simply crossed by a few black lines, one perpendicular and two horizontal, for example, marking-off planes calculated to the tenth of a millimetre, then the picture is the very image of pure rhythm and perfect harmony.

Ills 139, 141–3

126 *Large Composition with Red, Blue and Yellow* 1928

127 *Composition with Red, Yellow and Blue* 1922

How did an artist who had been so influenced by cubism arrive at such results? He gave his own explanation in talks to J.J. Sweeney only a few weeks before his death:

'The intention of cubism – in any case in the beginning – was to express volume. Three-dimensional space – natural space – thus remained. Cubism therefore remained basically a naturalistic expression and was only *an abstraction* – not true abstract art.

'This attitude of the cubists to the representation of volume in space was contrary to my conception of abstraction, which

128
Composition III
1929

is based on the belief that this very space *has* to be destroyed. As a consequence I came to the destruction of volume by the use of the plane. This I accomplished by means of lines cutting the planes. But still the plane remained too intact. So I came to making only lines and brought the colour within the lines. Now the only problem was to destroy these lines also through mutual oppositions.

'Perhaps I do not express myself clearly in this, but it may give some idea why I left the cubist influence. True Boogie-Woogie I conceive as homogeneous in intention with mine in painting; destruction of melody which is the equivalent of destruction of natural appearance; and construction through the continuous opposition of pure means – dynamic

129
Fox Trot B
1929

rhythm. I think the destructive element is too much neglected in art.'

In order to eliminate all sense of depth Mondrian went so far as to not allow any kind of frame for his pictures. Again, speaking to J. J. Sweeney, he said: 'So far as I know, I was the first to bring the painting forward from the frame, rather than set it within the frame. I had noted that a picture without a frame works better than a framed one, and that framing causes sensations of three dimensions. It gives an illusion of depth, so I took a frame of plain wood and mounted my picture on it. In this way I brought it to a more real existence.'

This determination to destroy space and depth led him at the same time to reject light, at least light as it had been conceived

130
Composition in a Square with Red, Yellow and Blue 1926

from the Renaissance to impressionism – the light of Caravaggio, the chiaroscuro of Rembrandt, the luminism of Claude Monet – used to create a specifically pictorial, subjective reality.

A system of expression so rigidly defined might appear easy to apply, but this was evidently not so, for the works of

131
Composition
with Black and Blue 1926

Van Doesburg, Huszar and other neo-plasticists are marked by a monotony, an aridity entirely foreign to those of their master. Let us take the series of lozenge-shaped canvases *(Compositions in the Square)* started in 1918. These lozenges permit the artist, by drawing straight lines *which are not parallel to the edges*, to divide his canvas into truncated squares and

triangles. He began by colouring them yellow, or red, or blue, but from 1926 onward he used only black and white, a combination which, contrary to what one might expect, proved infinitely richer and more powerful than the primary colours. In fact, by using only straight lines intersecting at right-angles, he was led to produce an arrangement of colourless squares which, being cut by one or more sides of the canvas, leave the spectator's imagination to complete their
Ill. 123 outlines *(Fox-Trot A,* 1927, Yale University, New Haven). In other cases, the lozenge carries only two lines intersecting on one of its lower sides. In one canvas, dated 1933, four yellow lines describe isosceles triangles in each of its four
Ill. 165 corners (Gemeentemuseum, The Hague).

132
Composition 1929

133 *Composition in a Square* 1929

Diversity is produced also by the number, arrangement and thickness of the lines which are, of course, always vertical or horizontal, never diagonal. It will be recalled that it was because Van Doesburg, in 1924, introduced obliques into his compositions that Mondrian broke off his connection with *De Stijl*. He considered Van Doesburg to have betrayed the sacrosanct dogma of neo-plasticism. In 1938, when he was told that Vantongerloo, who had been one of the earliest members of the *De Stijl* team, was using curves, he replied, with a grimace of bitter disapproval, 'I might have known!'

134 *Composition with Red, Yellow and Blue* 1927

MOVEMENT WITHIN STABILITY

An aspect of Mondrian's art which has not received the attention it deserves, although he himself made no attempt to conceal it, was related to James J. Sweeney in 1949.

'It is important to discern two sorts of equilibrium in art: 1. static balance, 2. dynamic equilibrium. And it is understandable that some advocate equilibrium, others oppose it. The great struggle for artists is the annihilation of static equilibrium in their paintings through continuous oppositions (contrasts) among the means of expression. It is always natural for human beings to seek static balance. This balance of course is necessary to existence in time. But vitality in the continual succession of time always destroys this balance. Abstract art is a concrete expression of such a vitality.

'Many appreciate in my former work just what I did not want to express, but which was produced by an incapacity to express what I wanted to express – *dynamic movement in equilibrium*. But a desperate struggle has brought me nearer to this goal. This is what I am attempting in *Victory Boogie-Woogie*. *Ill. 205*

'Doesburg, in his late work, tried to destroy static expression by a diagonal arrangement of the lines in his compositions. But through such an emphasis the feeling of physical equilibrium which is necessary for the enjoyment of a work of art is lost.

'If a square picture, however, is hung diagonally, as I have frequently planned my pictures to be hung, this effect does not result. Only the borders of the canvas are at 45° angles, not the picture. The advantage of such a procedure is that longer horizontal and vertical lines may be employed in the composition.'

And so, far from having intended to produce a static painting, Mondrian applied himself to expressing what he called 'dynamic movement in equilibrium', that is, dynamism in stability, movement in calm, and consequently emotion underlying apparent impassivity. Although he tried to attain the permanent and the universal, he was not aware that permanency is in perpetual movement, that the universe is eternally in a process of transformation, an endless alternation of creation and destruction, and that universal equilibrium is unceasingly being challenged by the passage of time. There is nothing more paradoxical in this than in the philosophy of Heraclitus, and the vitality invoked by Mondrian makes it impossible not to recall the 'rhythmical vitality'

135
Composition
1930

136 *Composition* 1931

which, for the ancient sages of China, was that very essence of things with which they considered they should impregnate their souls. To put the matter more simply, we might say that, however rigid his intellectualism, however resolute his anti-romanticism, it was at no time Mondrian's intention to cut himself off from life, but, on the contrary, always to put the very essence of life into his work.

'The first aim in a painting', he said in the interview with J.J. Sweeney from which we have already quoted, 'should be universal expression. What is needed in a picture to realize this is an equivalence of vertical and horizontal expressions.

137
Composition I
1930

138
Composition with Yellow
1930

139
Composition I with Black Lines
1930

This I feel today I did not accomplish in such early works as my 1911 *Tree* paintings. In those the vertical emphasis predominated. A "Gothic" expression was the result.

'The second aim should be concrete, universal expression. In my work of 1919 and 1920 (where the surface of the canvas was covered by adjoining rectangles) there was an equivalence of horizontal and vertical expression. Thus the whole was more universal than those in which verticals predominated. But this expression was vague. The verticals and horizontals cancelled each other, the result was confused, the structure was lost.

140 *Composition with Red, Black and White* 1931

141 *Composition 2 with Black Lines* 1930

'In my paintings after 1922 I feel that I approached the concrete structure I regard as necessary. And in my latest pictures such as *Broadway Boogie-Woogie* and *Victory Boogie-Woogie* the structure and means of expression are both concrete and in mutual equivalence.'

Ills 207, 20

142
Composition I A 1930

An artist's pronouncements about himself are never, however lucid he may be, entirely free from error. In Mondrian's case, one might certainly suppose that, if vertical and horizontal lines were at the same time necessary and sufficient for him to create a work unequalled in the history of western painting, he must occasionally have felt that this work was threatened with excessive aridity, and that by skirting the

143
Composition with Two Lines 1931

brink of the void he was running the risk of falling into it, though not entirely unwillingly, like the anchorites of Asia who allowed themselves to be absorbed, in beatitude, into the indeterminate state of nirvana.

The fact remains that he began, from 1922 onwards, to duplicate his perpendiculars. Later, he increased the number of parallels which, by cutting one another at right-angles, gave his canvases the appearance of grids, illuminated here and there with tiny rectangles of colour. It was a similar, *Ills 205, 207* though much bolder, move that gave rise to his *Boogie-Woogie* series, painted in New York in 1942–44.

And yet, however austere, however cold his painting may appear at first sight, it is far from lifeless. Reduced to the most elementary figures and colours, to the simplest geometrical forms, Mondrian, in his painting, has condensed a seething mass of forces, compressed an accumulation of energy, and mastered perfectly the occult powers of the universe. It might, indeed, almost explode if he did not, at the crucial moment, solicit the intervention of the spectator to complete what he has suggested.

144
Composition D with Red, Yellow and Blue
1932

145 *Composition with Blue and Yellow* 1932

Mondrian is inhuman only to those who prefer the picturesque, the eloquent, the tragic, and are impressed only by outbursts of passion and displays of emotion. 'The creations of genius', it has been said, 'are chilling; not because genius is lacking in warmth, but because, by its inventions, it disconcerts perceptions blunted by habit and routine.'

In Paris, Mondrian discovered, through cubism, the course he was to follow. During the twenty-odd years he lived there, he was able to work out and finally perfect the principles of neo-plasticism, and it was in Paris that he executed his master works. When he returned to Paris in 1919, he settled once more in the Rue du Départ in the studio his friend Conrad Kickert had lent him in 1912. When Kickert reclaimed the studio, Mondrian moved to some rooms in the Rue de Coulmiers, near the Porte d'Orléans, where he remained until 1921, when he went back to the same house in the Rue du Départ, though to another studio two floors below his friend Kickert's. In his book *Les Feux de Montparnasse,* Anatole Jakovsky has described the place where Mondrian

146
Composition A
1932

147
Composition B ith Grey and Yellow
1932

lived for fifteen years as a place from which 'nature was banned, and [where] the light was almost completely artificial. The only window in the place was camouflaged, and such daylight as was able to penetrate was filtered to the point of seeming almost unreal. Everywhere, including on the walls, which were quite high, were set out, in an order that was balanced and cunningly calculated beyond perfection, a few squares of yellow and red and blue against vast stretches of white. The gramophone was red; so was the table. The wardrobe was blue. The plates yellow. The curtains red. Everything else was painted dead white, making the place into a kind of operating-theatre for extracting the square roots of the rainbow. It was a kind of materialization of the *Discours de la méthode* of colour.'

148
Composition with Blue and Red
1933

Jakovsky's account of this very individual workplace is confirmed by the more detailed description given by Michel Seuphor in his study of Mondrian:

'The room was quite large, very bright, with a very high ceiling. Mondrian had divided it irregularly, utilizing for this purpose a large black-painted cupboard, which was partially hidden by an easel long out of service; the latter was covered with big red, grey and white pasteboards. Another easel rested against the large rear wall whose appearance changed often, for Mondrian applied to it his neo-plastic virtuosity. The second easel was completely white, and used only for showing finished canvases. The actual work was done on the table. It stood in front of the large window facing the Rue du Départ, and was covered with a canvas waxed white and nailed to the under side of the boards. I often surprised Mondrian there, armed with a ruler and ribbons of

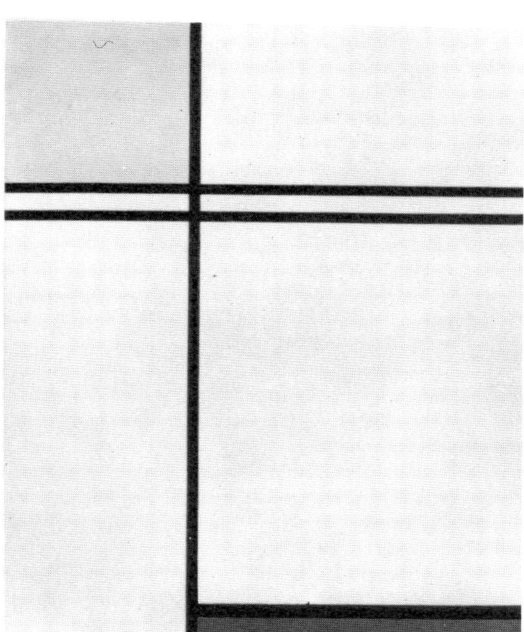

149
Composition with Blue and Yellow
1933

transparent paper, which he used for measuring. I never saw him with any other working tool... He had two large wicker armchairs, also painted white, and on the scrupulously clean floor, two rugs, one red, the other grey. Such was the studio where Mondrian lived for thirteen years, where he received so many visitors, where he painted his most "classical" works, the ones most justly admired, and where he also suffered a great deal from solitude, illness, poverty.'

His poverty was genuine. According to Seuphor, Mondrian had left with his friend Simon Maris (the son of Willem Maris, one of the masters of the Hague school of painters) almost his entire output previous to 1911, in particular the canvases painted in Brabant and Zeeland. He attached little importance to these early figurative works and allowed them to be sold for next to nothing. When he went over entirely to neo-plasticism he could find no buyers for his abstract compositions, though there was one Dutch writer who would have bought three of them – if only he had been able to muster the necessary hundred florins!

Between 1922 and 1925, at the request of Salomon Slijper, Mondrian agreed, rather reluctantly, to paint flowers in watercolour. They are very similar to the flowers he had painted in 1907–10, and not much better in their execution. A concession such as this must have been hard for an artist as proud and intransigent as Mondrian. Having to earn his living by doing work he disapproved of must have made him hate all the flowers in creation. Indeed that would seem to be a good explanation of Michel Seuphor's assertion that he had never seen a real flower in Mondrian's studio. All he had seen was an artificial tulip whose equally artificial leaf Mondrian had painted white, in order to 'banish entirely from his studio any reminder of the green he found so intolerable'.

It is true that, at a certain point in his life, Mondrian began to loathe anything green – trees, plants, meadows – to such an extent that, according to the Dutch critic Jos de Gruyter *(De Europese Schilderkunst na 1850)*, when on a train he would draw the blinds in his compartment in order not to see the trees. Michel Seuphor, too, tells how, when he was invited to lunch with Albert Gleizes, who lived on the Boulevard Lannes, Mondrian asked to change places at table so as to sit with his back to the trees in the Bois de Boulogne. He did the same thing at Kandinsky's in Neuilly, and when he visited Arp at Meudon. In his later years, Mondrian was glad to be living in New York, saying he found Paris far too romantic 'with all those avenues of trees'. The grasslands of his native country also lost their appeal, and may even have contributed something to his decision never to return to Holland.

An aversion of this kind is surprising, particularly when one thinks of the unforgettable series of *Trees*, his favourite

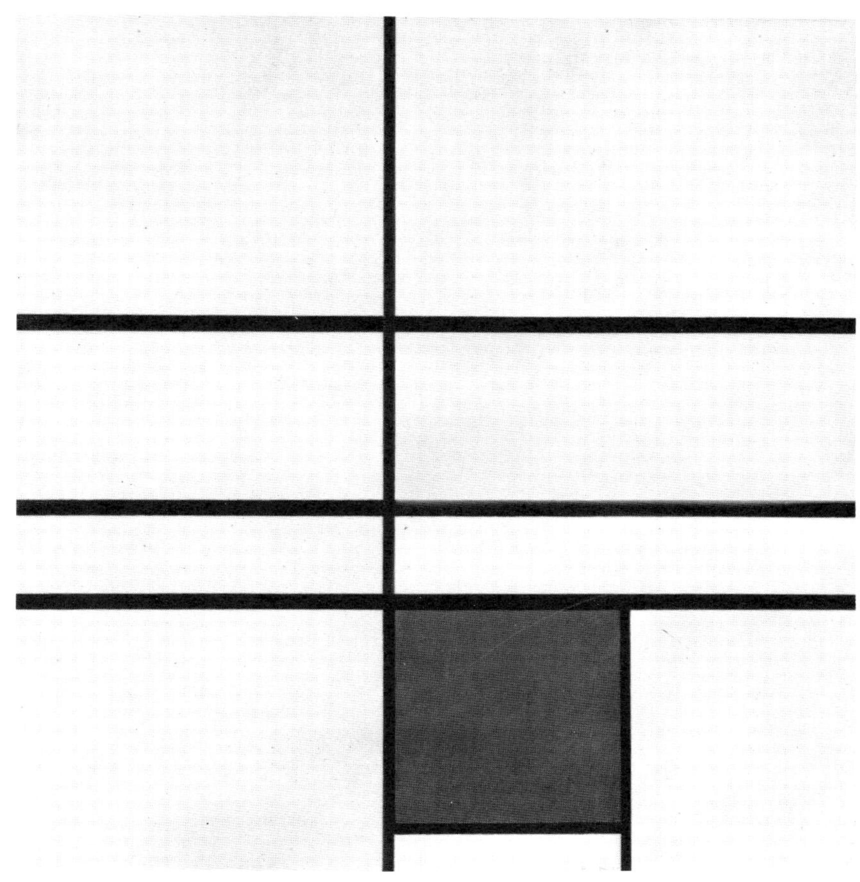

150 *Composition with Blue* 1935

theme for four years (1908–12), and now regarded as one of the glories of his work. But in fact this *volte-face* is inseparable from the revolution which took place in the artist's thought about 1912, when, having forsworn naturalism, he channelled all his powers into non-figurative work and pursued his object with such urgent conviction, such inflexible will-power, that everything that could remind him of his past became inevitably unbearable.

Besides, entirely absorbed as he was in his task, concentrating for weeks and months on a single picture, in search of that supreme perfection beyond which it is humanly impossible to go, Mondrian averted his gaze and his mind from everything likely to distract him from his labours. Anatole Jakovsky relates how he once met Mondrian in the street on one of those balmy, enervating days so typical of Paris in the spring, and complained to him about being unable to work. The answer he got was this: 'Reason takes no account of the seasons. The only things that count are one's mind and one's work. So far as I'm concerned, spring has long since ceased to exist.'

151
Composition with Red and Black
1936

152 *Composition* 1935

DISAPPOINTMENTS AND CONSOLATIONS

A small pamphlet, *Le Néo-Plasticisme,* written by Mondrian and printed at his own expense, was published in 1920 under the patronage of Léonce Rosenberg, the well-known art dealer who, at that time, was running the gallery known as L'Effort Moderne in the Rue de la Baume. The French in which this somewhat abstruse text is written was too uncertain to hold the attention of any would-be readers, and so the work passed unnoticed. In November 1923 Mondrian was again disappointed. An exhibition organized at Rosenberg's gallery by the *De Stijl* group was a fiasco. However,

153
Composition with Red and Blue
1936

in 1925, Mondrian was somewhat vindicated, when the Weimar Bauhaus published *Die neue Gestaltung,* an excellent German translation of the pamphlet published in Paris in 1920, and now augmented by articles he had published in a number of periodicals. This little book, more than anything else, helped to make the author known in Germany. By 1926 his renown had spread to the United States. A rich, perspicacious American collector, Katherine S. Dreier, sought him out and bought *Composition: Lozenge in Black and White* which she later donated to the Museum of Modern

Ill. 117

Art in New York. This canvas was shown the same year at the International Exhibition organized in Brooklyn by the Société Anonyme, an association devoted to the promotion of modern art in the United States, and of which Miss Dreier was a founder-member. Later, again in the same year, she bought several more of Mondrian's paintings. Her action was imitated by A. E. Gallatin, founder of the Museum of Living Art in Philadelphia, as well as by collectors in Germany and Switzerland.

From then on, Mondrian no longer needed to paint flowers. Although he lost his customers in Holland, they remained loyal to him as friends and admirers. His ideas were beginning

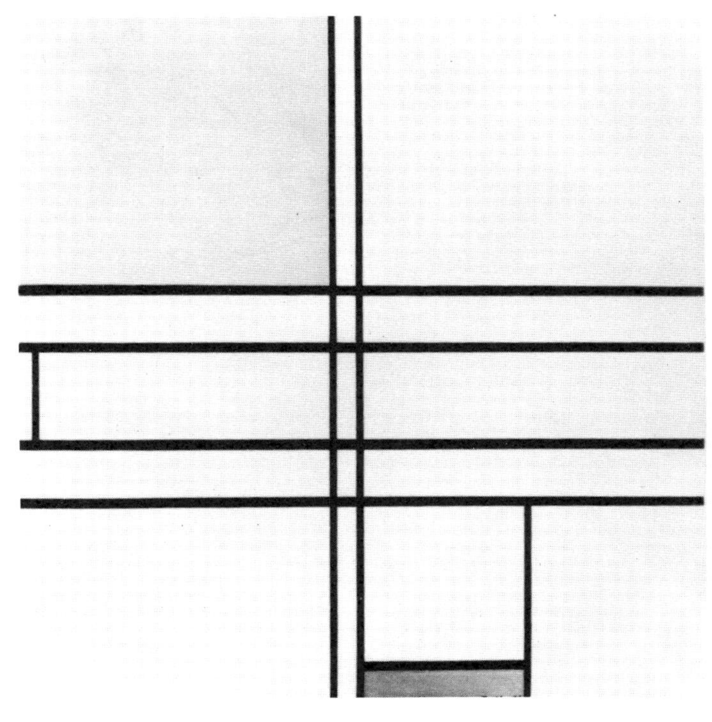

154
Composition with Blue and Yellow
1936

to spread beyond a narrow circle of enthusiasts. His works were no longer completely unknown to the Parisian public. At an exhibition called 'L'Art d'Aujourd'hui', organized by Poznanski at the headquarters of the Syndicat des Antiquaires in December 1925, Mondrian was represented by a number of his latest compositions. This particular exhibition included, besides the complete *De Stijl* group, cubists, futurists, the orphists Robert and Sonia Delaunay, the Bauhaus artists Klee and Moholy-Nagy and the purists Ozenfant and Le Corbusier. It was the first exhibition in which abstract painting made a major impact.

In April 1930 the Cercle et Carré (Circle and Square) group, founded the previous year by Michel Seuphor and Torrès-Garcia, exhibited, at Galerie 23, Rue La Boétie, about a hundred non-figurative canvases, including, besides works by Mondrian, Arp, Sophie Taeuber, Kandinsky, Vantongerloo, Schwitters, Huszar, Pevsner and Vordemberge-Gildewart, paintings by a number of young artists recently converted to the new art. The group was disbanded and its magazine, also called *Cercle et Carré*, ceased publication after its third issue, when Michel Seuphor fell seriously ill.

By the time Michel Seuphor returned to Paris after convalescing in Grasse, Herbin and Vantongerloo had reassembled the main elements of the Cercle et Carré group into an association called Abstraction-Création, over which Mondrian, by the mere fact of his membership, exercised considerable authority. After contributing to the magazine
Ill. 155 *Cercle et Carré*, he continued to write for the albums published by the new group, the last of which appeared in 1936.

Michel Seuphor was born in Antwerp in 1901 and went to Paris in 1923. There he very soon made contact with Mondrian, in whom he had discovered the artist who, by his intellectual integrity and his quest for a rigorously exacting

Ne pas s'occuper de la
forme et de la couleur – en-
tant-que-forme, c'est
en art, la nouvelle plas-
tique –
ne pas être trop dominé
par le physique-naturel,
c'est la nouvelle menta-
lité.
Compter exclusivement
avec les rapports en les cré-
ants et en cherchant leur
équilibre en art et dans la
vie, c'est le beau travail
d'aujourd'hui: c'est
préparer l'avenir.

dec. 29. Piet Mondrian

155 Mondrian's manuscript for a short contribution to the first issue of *Cercle et Carré*, Paris 1930 (see p. 251)

style, was capable of re-thinking and renewing the art of painting. Seuphor had literary leanings – he wrote essays and poems – but he now began to paint in gouache and to produce 'unilinear' drawings. And Mondrian immediately decided the young Anversois was worthy of his confidence. Seuphor corrected Mondrian's French, listened to his talk and helped to spread his ideas. Until 1934 Seuphor was not only Mondrian's disciple but his confidant as well. The Ill. 156 *Tableau-Poème,* dated 1928 (Michel Seuphor Collection, Paris), which consists of a poem by Seuphor written into a composition by Mondrian, an *oeuvre de circonstance* he nevertheless executed with great attention to detail, is a touching proof of their friendship.

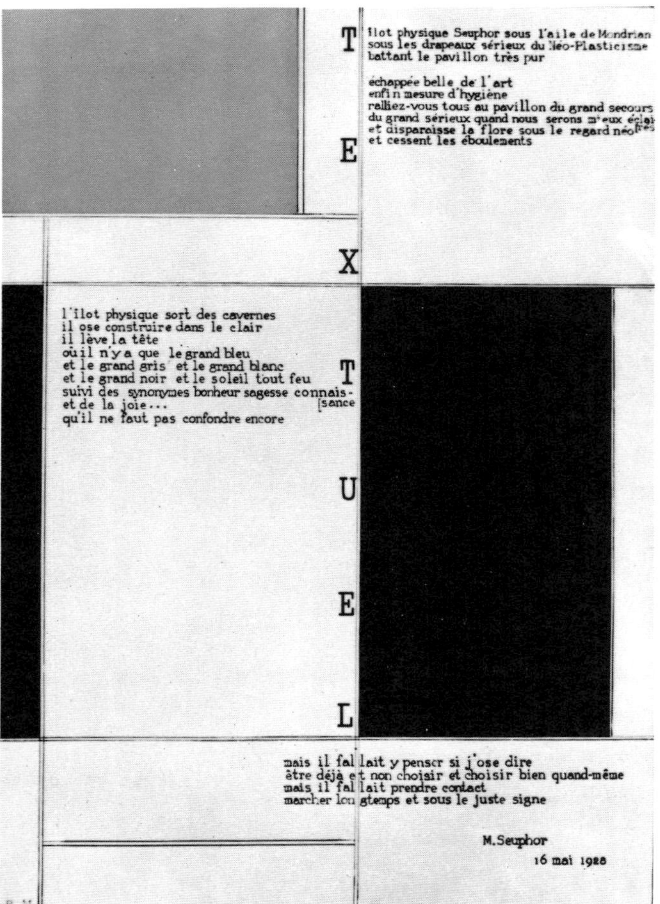

156
Tableau-Poème
with Michel Seuphor
1928
(see p. 251)

157 *Composition with Red and Black* 1927

When, after an absence of fourteen years, Seuphor at last returned from the provinces to Paris, Mondrian had already been dead for four years. Seuphor then decided to follow Mondrian's tracks through Holland and the United States, to meet people who had known him, and visit the places

158
Composition B with Red
1935

where he had worked. Thus started a quest, the outcome of which was the publication in 1956 of his now famous monograph, to which he has added other writings and lectures on abstract art, in all of which Mondrian's work is discussed and set up as an example. If we are now able to see Mondrian in his full stature, it is thanks, first and foremost, to the work of Michel Seuphor.

Jakovsky reports that while he was working Mondrian liked to listen, not only to Bach, but also to ragtime jazz. 'They connect', he used to say. And Jakovsky adds, 'he loved

159
Composition III with Blue and Yellow
1936

0 *Composition with Red* 1936

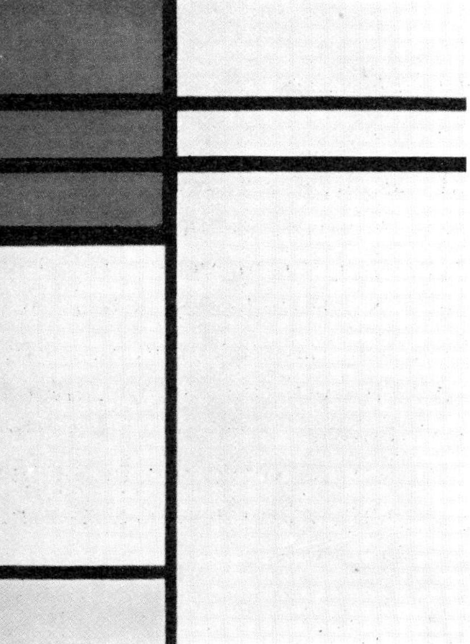

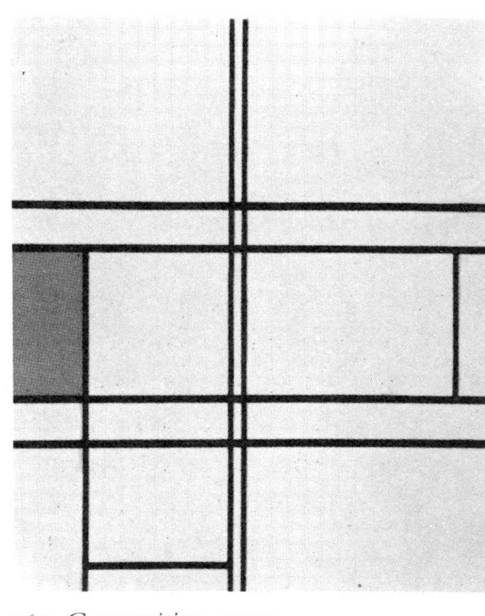

161 *Composition* 1935

162 *Composition with Red, Yellow and Blue* 1928

jazz and young women, and, despite his advanced age, he liked to dance, and used to go, *sub rosa,* to the cheap local dance-halls.' The latter part of that statement is probably closer to fiction than to truth. Nevertheless Seuphor also speaks of Mondrian's fondness for dancing, and says the greatest pleasure one could give him was to take him, after a good meal, to a dance-hall. Mondrian certainly took the pastime very seriously, and we know, through one of his contemporaries, that as early as 1918, when he was at Laren,

163 *Composition with Red, Blue and Yellow* 1930

he used to go dancing every Sunday. His passion for it was so real that he criticized his native country when he heard, in 1928, that it had banned the Charleston for being too suggestive. He was quite prepared to look upon the ban, if it had been maintained, as an amply sufficient reason for refusing ever to set foot again on Dutch soil. His love of dancing remained steadfast to the end of his life. His two last canvases were, in fact, deeply inspired by what was then the latest and most dynamic of dances – the boogie-woogie.

In 1936, when the house in the Rue du Départ was expropriated, Mondrian moved to a more spacious and comfortable studio at 278 Boulevard Raspail. But, like most elderly bachelors, he found it difficult to get used to a change of habits and surroundings, and never felt settled there. So when, two years later, the growing menace of Hitler made him decide to quit the Continent altogether, he left the new studio without regrets.

Mondrian's reactions to approaching war were typical; he saw it less as a collective misfortune than as a personal affront, an intolerable cause of turmoil that would disturb, and possibly destroy the well-ordered universe he had created and of which he himself was the centre. By the end of the summer of 1938 he was already thinking of taking refuge in London. In 1934, and again in 1936, he had met Ben Nicholson and, in spite of the twenty years' difference in their ages, they had got on well together. It was through the person of Ben Nicholson, therefore, that, distressed and perturbed by the events leading up to the war, he first felt drawn towards England.

Nicholson himself has described their first meeting in terms which suggest the atmosphere of respectful admiration which surrounded Mondrian at that time. 'I remember', he writes, 'sitting at a café table on the edge of the pavement almost touching all the traffic going in and out of the Gare Montparnasse, and sitting there for a very long time with an astonishing feeling of quiet and repose . . . The thing I remembered most was the feeling of light in his room and the pauses and the silences during and after he'd been talking. The feeling in his studio must have been not unlike the feeling in one of those hermits' caves where lions used to go to have thorns taken out of their paws.'

164 *Composition with Blue* 1937

On 21 September 1938, Mondrian left Paris never to return. In London, Ben Nicholson and the sculptor Naum Gabo, who had settled in Britain two years previously, found him a large room at 60, Park Hill Road, Hampstead, quite close to their own studios, and not far from Barbara Hepworth's. This new home Mondrian equipped with white painted furniture. The terrible irony was that, having left Paris because he was sure it would be destroyed by the *Luftwaffe*, he found that London was the target. Harry Holtzman, a very young American painter, who had also met Mondrian in Paris, and had great admiration for him, urged

165 *Composition with Yellow Lines* 1933

him to go to the United States. He even offered him the money for his fare. But to no effect. In spite of the bombs showering London, the infernal din of explosions and gunfire, and the ear-piercing wailing of sirens, Mondrian was determined not to budge. But when the house next to his was destroyed

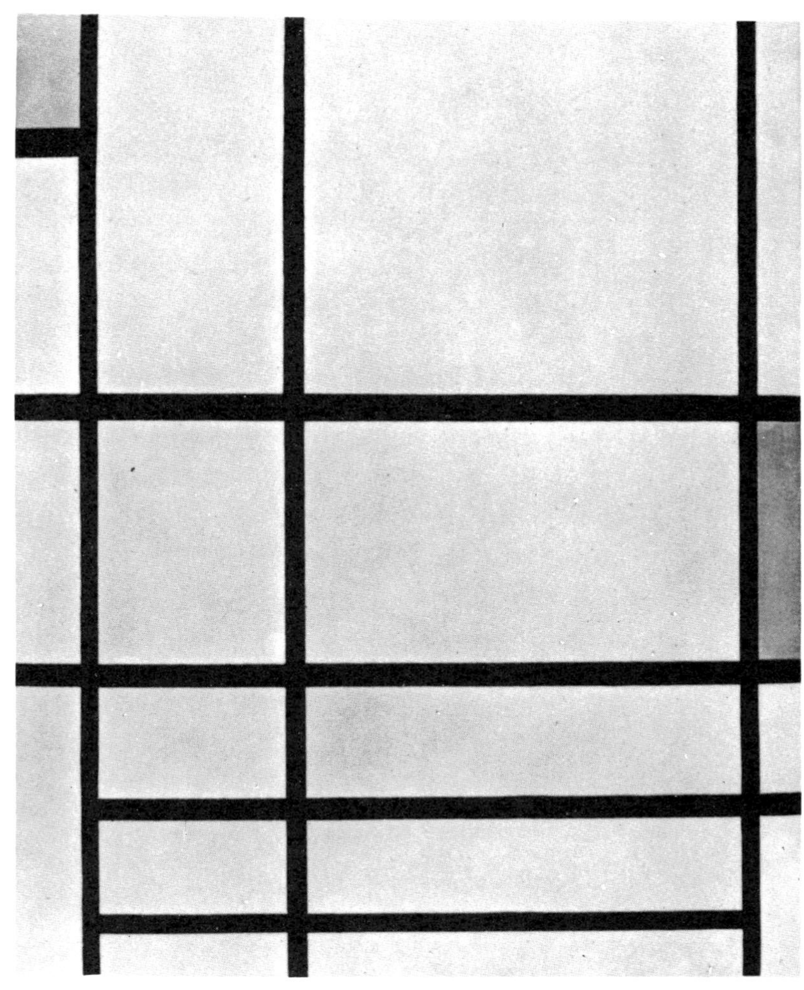

166 *Composition 2 with Red and Blue* 1937

by a bomb, all his friends, particularly Barbara Hepworth, urgently advised him to accept Harry Holtzman's repeated offers. He sailed from England on 20 September 1940, leaving behind his devoted friends and the patrons he had found there in the previous two years.

CHAPTER SIX

The final years

Worn out, but delighted, Mondrian arrived in New York on 3 October, followed, a little later, by his canvases. In a few weeks, thanks to the generous hospitality of his American friends, he had recovered from his fatigue and anxiety. Instead of feeling out of place in the New World, he found its atmosphere somehow familiar. It is here, he thought, that the civilization and the culture of the future were to be fashioned; here, too, more than anywhere else, neo-plasticism would have every chance. Far from being overwhelmed by the Dantesque spectacle of New York, he felt reassured by it. The straight lines of the streets, the verticals of the skyscrapers, the rectangles of the windows infinitely repeated in the long lines of the façades, were the image, cast in steel and concrete, of the scheme that had for so long occupied his mind. They were the tangible reflection of his inmost self.

He first settled in an apartment on First Avenue, not far from many leading New York galleries. He was even closer to them when he moved some time later to East 89th Street. The following description of his first New York studio was given in an article in the *Journal of Aesthetics and Art Criticism*, by Charmion von Wiegand, herself an artist strongly influenced by Mondrian's work: 'On the walls hang sketches. On one wall rectangles of blue, red, and yellow. Red predominates. The sketches are old, on yellowing paper, done in charcoal, ink, or pencil. There is a table, one stool with a

167 Mondrian's studio in New York. On the easel, *Victory Boogie-Woogie*

bright red plastic seat and a pair of ordinary stools. Not one item of "bourgeois" furniture. Not one ornament.'

Charmion von Wiegand has also provided some valuable details about the artist himself and his methods of work. She tells us, for example, that, far from proceeding by analysis or by deduction, Mondrian let himself be guided by intuition. He used no measuring instruments, but relied entirely on the eye. 'He tests each picture over a long period by eye,' she writes. 'It is a physical adjustment of proportion through training, intuition and testing.' She then tells how Mondrian showed her a picture that had been exhibited at the Riverside Museum, a square canvas with black lines, on which he had traced, very faintly in charcoal, a thin line beside one of the

168 *Composition with Red* 1937

rectangles. 'He explained,' she says, 'that when he saw this canvas in the exhibition he felt that two lines near the edge of the canvas needed widening; he intends to repaint them half a centimetre broader. To my eyes, this made only the slightest difference; but he is so extraordinarily sensitive to the laws of proportion that, to him, it seemed of the highest importance.'

The setting Mondrian needed to work in was far too important to him for his second New York studio to have been noticeably different from his first one. Fritz Glarner has left us some excellent photographs which give us a very clear idea

169 *Composition with Yellow, Blue and White* 1937

of the kind of places they were, as well as of the man who lived in them. They show the same monastic simplicity which he always preferred. The walls, as well as the wooden crates he used for furniture, are carefully painted white. The only things that stand out against the total, the supreme sobriety of this background are the famous squares of cardboard painted in the three primary colours, the components of his powerful alchemy. For, wherever he lived, he furnished and decorated in the same way, according to the principles of his doctrine. He could have lived equally easily in any town in the world, so long as he had a room arranged according to

170
Composition with Blue and Yellow
1937

these laws. His studio was like one of his pictures, just as each one of his pictures was drawn in his own image. He lived in it just as he lived in his work. It was the dwelling of a *grand solitaire,* but it was also the home of a man who, in a world of material profusion, refused to be enslaved by things.

In New York, Mondrian found, besides Harry Holtzman, Katherine S. Dreier, the Berlin artist Hans Richter, who had contributed to *De Stijl* between 1921 and 1925, and Alexander Calder, who had been a fellow-member, in Paris, of the Abstraction-Création group. He also made new friends, including, as well as some of the leading figures in the Dutch colony, Carl Holty, Peggy Guggenheim, A. E. Gallatin, the art-critic J. J. Sweeney and the dealer Valentin Dudensing, to whom he sold a number of pictures. Among the French wartime expatriates in New York he met Marcel Duchamp, Max Ernst, Fernand Léger and the surrealist writer André Breton.

171
Composition with Red and Yellow
1937

Mondrian's reputation continued to grow. His daily needs were now assured. He had, in fact, more money than he actually required, but that in no way altered the simplicity of his way of life. Physically, he had changed very little, in spite of his sixty-nine years. Behind his frail appearance it was still possible to recognize a vigour unimpaired. Although he had only two more years to live, his determination and his assiduity showed no sign of weakening. His canvases, new as well as those on which he had begun work in Paris and London, reveal his extraordinary need for renewal. In the *Ill. 177* *Composition with Red, Yellow and Blue* (1939–42, Harry Holtzman Collection, New York) just as much as in the other very different composition with the same title (1939–42, Donald O. Stewart Collection, New York) his work is bright with lively, original rhythms.

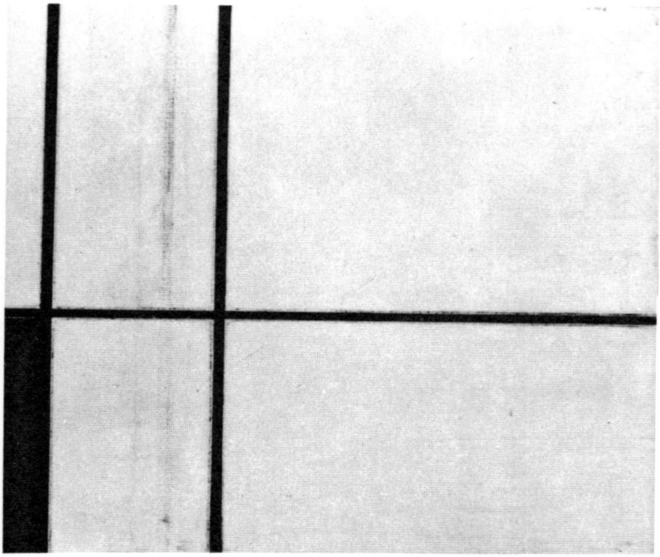

172
Composition with Blue
(unfinished)
c. 1938

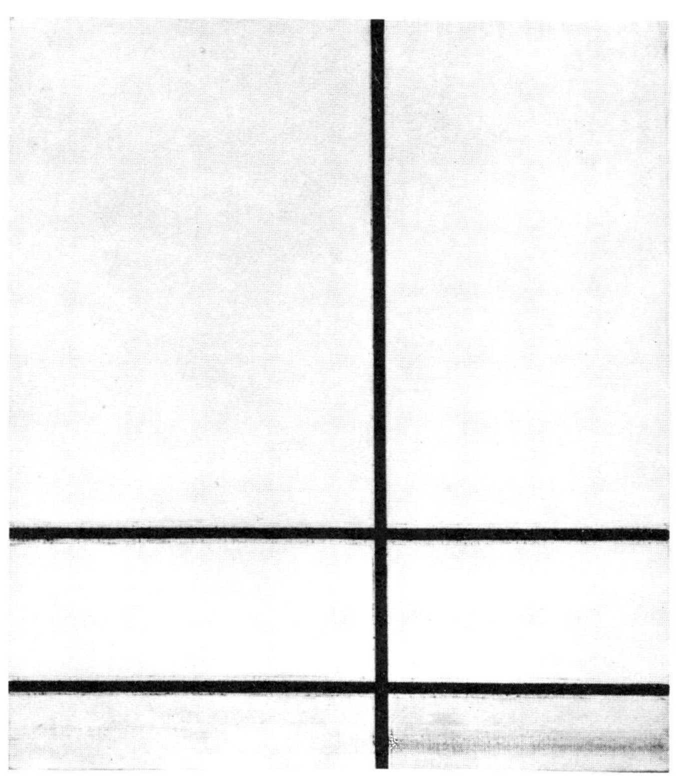

173
Composition
(unfinished)
1938

Again, one has only to look at *Place de la Concorde* (1938–43, Harry Holtzman Collection), or his *Trafalgar Square* (1939–43, John L. Senior Collection, New York), to be aware of the obvious desire to suggest the physiognomy of great modern cities, and perhaps to shape that of cities of the future as well. The same animation is evident in the *Composition in the Square, with Red Corner* (1943, J.J. Sweeney Collection, New York), a late continuation of the 'lozenges' of 1926–33, with its lines sharply cut off by the sides of the canvas. All these works were started before Mondrian went to America. Once there, he set to work on *New York* (1941–2) and *New York City* (1942, Sidney Janis Gallery), two

Ill. 196
Ill. 186
Ill. 198
Ill. 197

174 *Composition with Red* 1939

admirable canvases which directly foreshadow the style of
lls 205, 207 the various *Boogie-Woogies*.

In the presentation of these canvases one thing stands out: for the first time in twenty-five years, since the birth of neo-plasticism, Mondrian has given his pictures explicit titles, a fact which clearly indicates a new direction in his thought. On the other hand, if one looks closely at *New York City*

175 *Composition with Red* 1939

one can see that there has been some kind of change in expression, for there are no more black lines, no more coloured shapes. Squares and rectangles now appear only when the grey background of the canvas is divided up by red, yellow and blue perpendiculars. And, as they are crossed or superimposed, these lines inevitably determine a certain depth. Does this mean that Mondrian was deliberately renouncing

176 *Composition No. 7* 1937–42

one of the sacrosanct principles of his dogma – bi-dimensionality?

Ill. 207 In *Broadway Boogie-Woogie* (1942–3, Museum of Modern Art, New York) the horizontals and verticals lose their individual unity as they are punctuated, along their entire

177 *Composition with Red, Yellow and Blue* 1939–42

length, by little alternating squares of blue, red, yellow or grey. On some of the neutral surfaces enclosed by these broken lines Mondrian has painted what one might describe as 'variegated windows' which increase in number in *Victory* *Ill. 205*
Boogie-Woogie (Burton Tremaine Collection, Meriden),

178 *Rhythms with Black Lines* 1935–42

while the multi-coloured lines are broken up to the point of imperceptibility. This painting 'in the square' is the artist's last work. Started in 1943, it was unfinished when he died, and has come to be regarded as a work of outstanding importance.

Michel Seuphor likes to see in it a picture of New York by night, when, as he interprets it, the whole city with all its

179 *Composition with Red, Yellow and Blue* 1939–42

lights ablaze becomes an immense *Victory Boogie-Woogie.* *Ill. 205*
The metaphor is certainly worth noting. But, bearing in mind the precise title given by the artist to his work and the chromatic vibration running through it, there is good reason for seeing it as a dynamic transposition of American music by a great jazz enthusiast, which Mondrian, of course, was. He detested what he considered the over-melodious quality

and the excessively sentimental phrasing of European symphonic music just as wholeheartedly as he delighted in the acid sharpness of the brass and the percussive rhythms of Negro jazz.

NEW YORK

There is no doubt that New York made a deep impression on Mondrian, evident in his last paintings. The same thing was happening, at the same time, to Fernand Léger, who expressed it in terms which Mondrian himself would have understood. 'This is the apotheosis of vertical architecture,' he wrote, 'an elegance as original as it is uncontrived emerges from all this geometrical abstraction. Clamped between two angles of metal, ciphers and numbers rise rigidly skywards, held in check by the deforming perspective. A New World!

'Brooklyn! Its massive wharves an interplay of lights and shadows, the bridges with their projections of vertical, horizontal, oblique lines . . . New York coming to life in the light that gets gradually brighter as you penetrate further into the city . . . The beauty of New York at night is composed of these countless points of light and the ceaseless flashing of its sky-signs . . . New York, transparent, translucent, towering all red and blue and yellow, a spectacle unparalleled in its magic.'

It is certainly this 'new world' that Mondrian tried to record in his late compositions and, what is more, by means of his 'vertical-horizontal' method. But can one fail to see the coherence and the clarity of his system being undermined by the allusive realism of his intentions, by the hints of impressionism in his colouring, by the unexpected intervention of the third dimension into the space of his very last pictures?

180 *Composition with Yellow* 1935

For indeed his last works have neither the utter starkness, the austere architectural ordering, nor the limpidity which set their value on his earlier canvases. His work, which had had the hardness and the purity of a diamond, reveals, at the end,

181 *Composition* 1939–41

182 *Composition with Red, Yellow and Blue* 1936–43

imperfections, or, since we are speaking of diamonds, flaws. Colour was not his strong point. The less recourse he has to it, the more convincing he is.

It seems unfortunate, therefore, that he did not resist the temptation to transmit to his ill-named neo-plasticism the joys so amply provided by American life. The forty months he spent in New York were highly satisfactory in many ways. He held two exhibitions, one in January–February 1942, at the Valentine Gallery, run by Valentin Dudensing, the other in March–April 1943. They were the only one-man exhibitions held in his lifetime. In 1942 the Society of American Abstract Artists invited him to give a public reading of his essay *A New Realism,* which was later published in 1946. Stimulated by his associates, Mondrian wrote a number of essays: *Toward the True Vision of Reality, Pure Plastic Art* and *Abstract Art,* which were immediately published. He

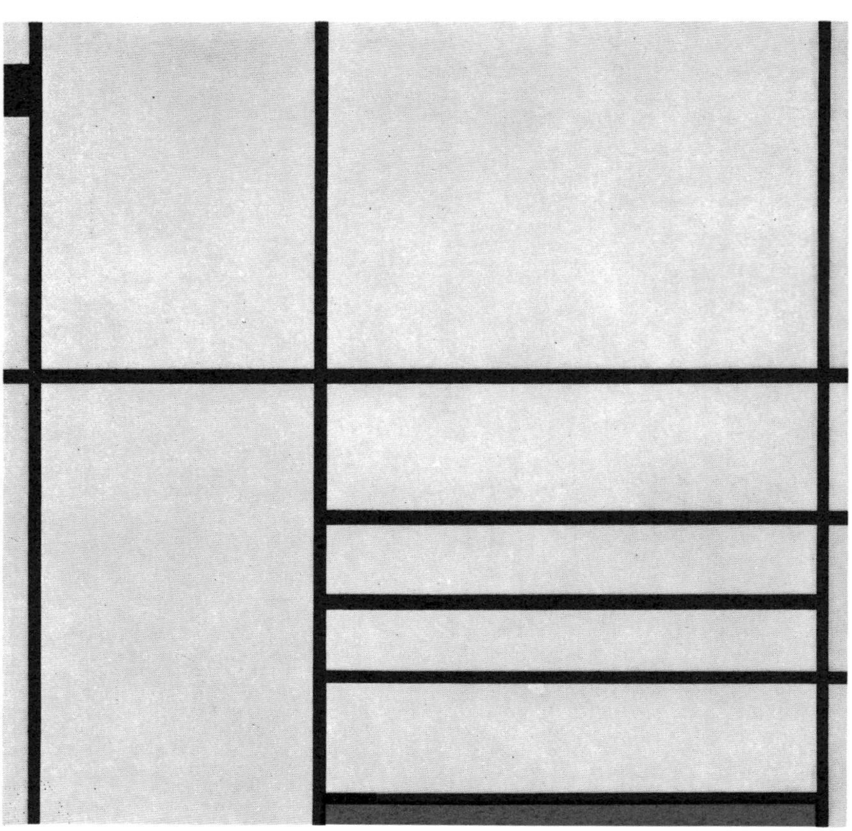

184 *Composition with Yellow Square* 1936

183 *Composition with Red and Black* 1936

enjoyed the friendship and deference of a wide circle of friends, including Harry Holtzman, Charmion von Wiegand, Fritz Glarner and Carol Holty, while the most influential members of the New York art world were unsparing in their encouragement. He became more and more apprecia-tive of American open-mindedness, and had decided to ask for naturalization. But his days were numbered. In January 1944 he caught a cold and developed pneumonia. On 26 January, when Fritz Glarner called at his studio, he found him in an alarming state of weakness. He at once informed

185
Composition
1939–42

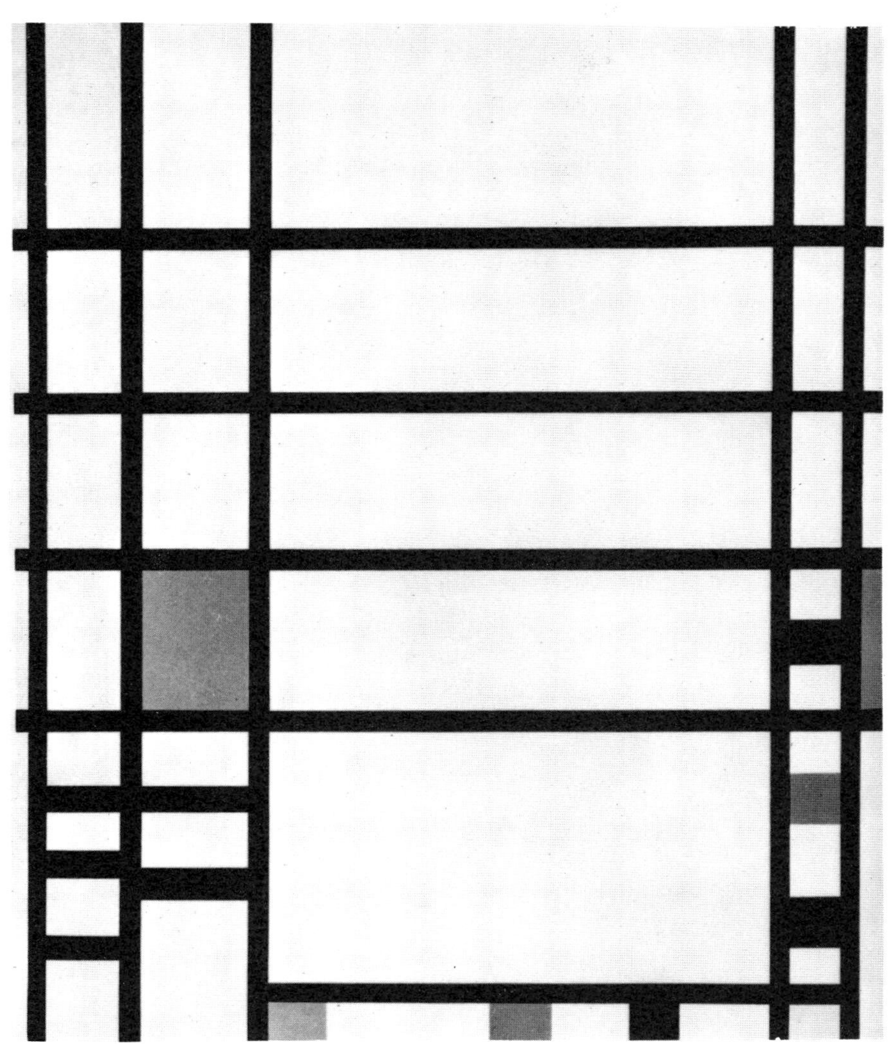

186 *Trafalgar Square* 1939–43

Harry Holtzman and a doctor was summoned who ordered the patient's immediate admission to Murray Hill Hospital. There Mondrian died on 1 February 1944, at the age of seventy-two.

187
Composition
with Red, Yellow and Blue
1935–42

188 *Composition* 1935–42

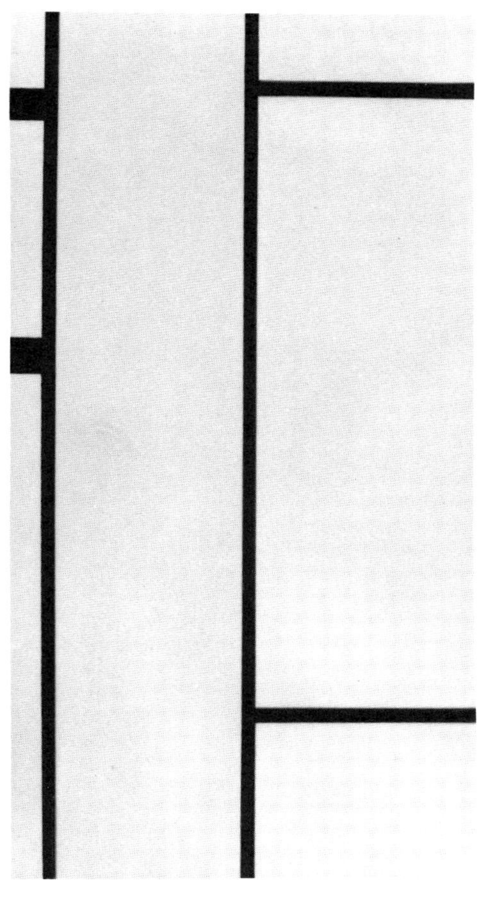

189
Composition 1935–42

He was buried on 3 February at Cypress Hill Cemetery, Brooklyn. Many people attended the funeral, including all his personal friends as well as European artists and intellectuals who had sought refuge in the United States. A religious service was held, and among those who addressed the gathering was Alfred Barr, the Director of The Museum of Modern Art, New York.

CHAPTER SEVEN

Conclusion

Because of the high esteem in which he was held, and the sympathy and admiration that surrounded Mondrian in America, it is there that a large number of his works are to be found, in both public and private collections. One of the most important, the Harry Holtzman Collection, includes not only much of his American work, but also pictures painted between 1922 and 1940. In Europe, the position is quite different; there, the creator of neo-plasticism, like his compatriots Jongkind and Van Gogh, met with almost complete indifference. The only notable exception is the Salomon B. Slijper Collection, at present on loan to the Gemeentemuseum, The Hague, which consists of some two hundred pictures, all painted before 1921. If to these we add the half-score of abstract paintings in the Kröller-Müller Museum at Otterlo, it is possible to get a coherent idea of the way in which Mondrian moved from traditional realism to geometrical abstraction.

It was only possible, however, to assess Mondrian's contribution to twentieth-century art and to the history of painting by assembling works from all his various periods which are presently scattered in the Dutch and American collections. This was done during the first half of 1966, first at Toronto, then in Philadelphia, and at the Gemeentemuseum at The Hague where a retrospective exhibition made it possible to trace the origins and development of one of the noblest minds that the world of art has ever known. This exhibition was

190 Poster of the retrospective exhibition at the Gemeentemuseum, The Hague, 1966. Illustrated with *Composition 2 with Black Lines*

exceptionally comprehensive and included works from Basle, Zurich, Brussels, Cologne and Stuttgart. These latter were few in number, it is true, for outside his native country, Europe is not rich in works by Mondrian. France does not possess a single canvas that does credit to the man who lived there for nearly a quarter of a century, exercised a profound influence and recruited disciples there, originating a style which made its mark on the decorative arts, advertising, industrial design, typography, window-dressing and even women's fashion. As recently as 1965, two Parisian couturiers successfully launched on the European market coats and dresses directly inspired by geometrical compositions, with the result that, in January 1966, at a fashion parade held in one of the rooms at the Gemeentemuseum, five models dressed *à la Mondrian* were seen by a crowded audience in a setting of Mondrian's canvases.

This kind of publicity would not have displeased Mondrian, who always wanted neo-plasticism to become part of everyday life. Did he not say that his ideal when he went over to abstract painting was 'to move the picture into our surroundings and give it a real existence'? As it is, his art has had to wait more than twenty years to merit the honour of a complete retrospective exhibition, while that other pioneer of abstract art, Kandinsky, who also died in 1944, was being enthusiastically and frequently honoured, particularly in France, where Mondrian still seems to be under an interdict.

MONDRIAN IN THE DEVELOPMENT OF ABSTRACT ART

The exact nature and extent of Mondrian's influence on western art is not easy to define. What influence he did have is inextricably linked with that of the Russian painter Malevich. Malevich, in Moscow, was probably the first to have the courage to exhibit a black square on a white ground. But he did not remain faithful to the dialectics of the square, which he claimed was his highest ideal. The founder of suprematism added to his arsenal the triangle, the circle and the cross. His work, however, has this in common with Mondrian's: they both intended to free themselves completely from the tyranny of the object. Of the two, it was the Dutch painter who systematized his conception, created a method, condensed into a simple relationship of lines the beauties which are dispersed through the world of objects, and succeeded, finally, by a series of constraints and sacrifices, in discovering the very essence of the creative mind.

Even when one accepts the bonds which united the theorists of suprematism and neo-plasticism, one finds it difficult to distinguish between the followers of Malevich and those of Mondrian. El Lissitzky, Vordemberge-Gildewart and

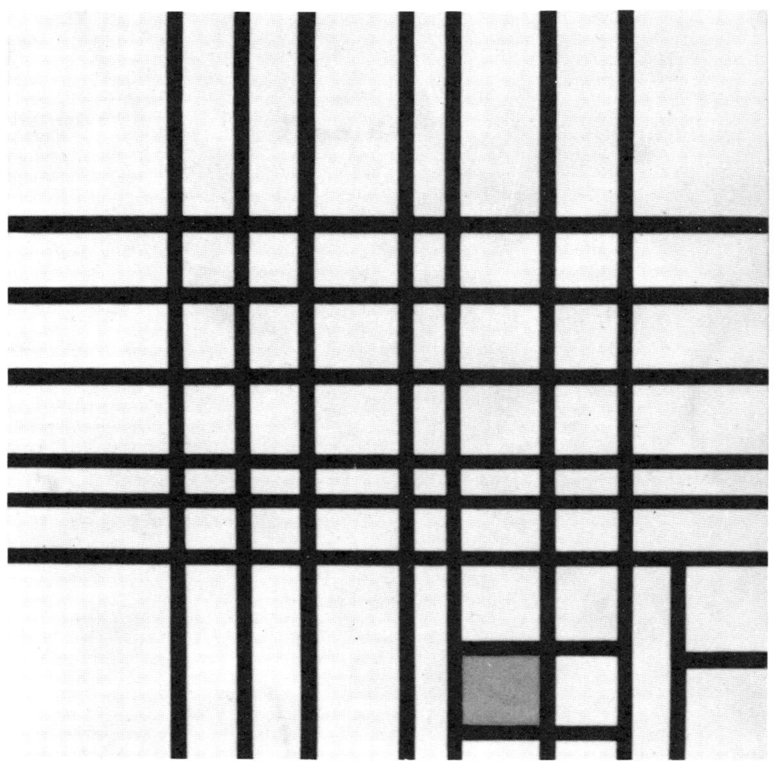

191 *Composition II with Blue* 1936–42

Albers, for example, seem to develop from the Russian artist. Diller and Glarner in the United States, Vantongerloo, Jean Gorin and Marcelle Cahn in France are confirmed disciples of neo-plasticism, although they all believe that the full expression of neo-plasticism calls for three dimensions, hence the projections into space of lines and planes of Vantongerloo and Gorin, and the addition of obliques, curves and circles to Mondrian's perpendiculars. *Ill. 194*

In a period characterized by a prodigious ferment of innovations and discoveries, Malevich and Mondrian were, with Kandinsky, the first promoters of abstraction in art.

True, a few other painters, notably Kupka, Delaunay and Léger, participated in this liberation movement, though with far less persistence, far less intransigence.

A few decorative compositions executed by Léger in 1924–6 show undeniable references to neo-plasticism. And it is to Mondrian, more than to any other painter, that artists, European and American, look for guidance if they practise any art that is reasoned, calculated, planned and geometrically constructed. It is Mondrian who is invoked when the moment comes to combat expressionist brutality and the excesses of lyrical abstraction, when hard edge and op' art set up in opposition to the frantic realism of the neo-dadaists, the neo-realists and 'pop-artists'.

Broadly speaking, the abstract painting movement split into two divergent currents, one derived from Kandinsky, the other from Mondrian. Kandinsky carried off the lyricals, the romantics, the effusionists; Mondrian the anti-romantics, the rationalists, the purists. Obviously the whole truth is much less arbitrary. For example, Kandinsky himself came under the direct influence of Mondrian during his period of teaching at the Bauhaus, founded by Gropius in Weimar in 1919, and where an active interest was taken in the ideas propagated by *De Stijl*.

In so far as they implied a renewal of structures and proportions, these ideas could not fail to have a resounding effect on the thought of architects and town-planners. Mondrian was fully aware of this. 'I feel,' he declared, 'that painting can become much more real, much less subjective, much more objective, when its possibilities are realized in architecture in such a way that the painter's capabilities are joined with constructive ones. But then the constructions would become very expensive; they would require a pretty long time for execution. I have studied the problem and practised the approach with movable colour and non-colour planes in several of my studios in Europe, just as I have done here in New York.'

The effectiveness of the vertical-horizontal rhythm did not fail to catch the imagination of architects. After Oud and Rietveld in Holland (both contributors to *De Stijl*), Gropius in Germany, Hoste and Bourgeois in Belgium, Le Corbusier in France, Sartoris in Switzerland and Mies van der Rohe in the United States, all showed that they were not unresponsive to the tenets of neo-plasticism.

The graphic and architectural predominance, so clear in the work of Mondrian, comes out too in the work of his immediate disciples and, though they are often more faithful to the spirit than the letter, in that of many European and American painters, including the Swiss artists Max Bill, *Ill. 192*
Lohsa, Graeser, and Honegger; the Belgians Servanckx,

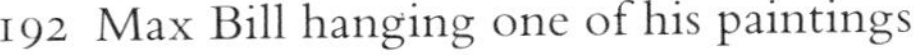
192 Max Bill hanging one of his paintings

193 Vasarely. *Manhattan* 1964

194
Fritz Glarner
Relational painting No. 70
1954

195
Ben Nicholson
White Relief
1939

Peeters, Closon and Luc Peire; the English painters Nicholson, Pasmore and Kenneth Martin; the Germans Leo Breuer, Fleischmann, Meistermann, Frühtrunk; the Italians Magnelli, Rho, Reggiani, Bonfanti; the Poles Stazewsi and Stizeminski, the Argentinian artist Pettoruti; Mortensen in Denmark, Baertling in Sweden, Picelj in Yugoslavia and, in France, Arp, Vasarely, Aurélie Nemours, Dewasne, Pillet, Folmer, Deyrolle among others and, finally, in the United States, Charmion von Wiegand, Glarner, L. P. Smith, John McLaughlin, Ellsworth Kelly, Noland, and Stella. *Ills 193–5*

Hans Richter, who had also worked on *De Stijl*, adopted the fundamental principles of neo-plasticism in his experimental films, and there are obvious reminders of Mondrian's way of thinking in the abstract films of the Canadian director, MacLaren. Alexander Calder has also acknowledged his debt to Mondrian for the inspiration of his mobiles. It was when he first saw Mondrian's compositions in the studio in the Rue du Départ, he says, that he had the idea of forms in constant motion in space.

THE ENIGMA OF MONDRIAN

Although Mondrian was our contemporary, and had friends, many of whom are still alive, although he wrote a great deal about his work and about himself, and exercised on the art of our time an influence as yet unequalled, his personality is still wrapped in mystery. It seemed to me essential, therefore, to collect all possible evidence which might throw light on certain episodes in his life, certain traits in his character and the motives behind his actions. Having done so, I find myself left, in spite of everything, with nothing more than a few hypotheses. I realize, for example, the weakness of the tentative explanation I have offered for Mondrian's apparent

196 *Place de la Concorde* 1938–43

loathing for nature, so profound that he could not even bear to look on vegetation, after having been so greatly attached to it for twenty-five years. All we really know is that after 1919, this artist, who once painted on the banks of the Amstel and the Gein and in the forest of Oele, who was so attracted by the landscapes of Brabant and Zeeland that he used to pay long and frequent visits to those parts, remained, so to speak, immured within his own studio.

197 *New York* 1941–2

When he was in Paris he never expressed the slightest desire to explore the surrounding countryside and showed no interest whatsoever in the French provinces.

When, at twenty-nine, he visited Spain with Simon Maris, he returned home disillusioned. After that he travelled abroad only when actually forced to do so. Yet, having left his native country in 1919, he never went back. Once he had settled in Paris, he would have stayed there for the rest of his life if the threat of war had not forced him to move to London. He would have ended his days in London if the German air raids had not driven him away. And even then, it needed the urgent entreaties of Harry Holtzman to make him agree to take refuge in New York. And once in New York, was he tempted to go out, even only so far as Long Island or along the banks of the Hudson? Not at all. During the forty months he spent in New York, I do not believe he ever went far beyond the quarter he actually lived in. As a background, all he needed was the white walls of his studio and, outside and around them, the buildings of a great city. What suited him much more than 'natural nature' was the second, artificial nature created by man.

In short, Mondrian was hardly more curious about the world than an anchorite in his cell. He trusted neither men nor things, fearing, one imagines, that they would lure him away from what he regarded as essential – his fanatical quest for absolute Beauty. I do not think he ever evinced the slightest interest in the painting of his illustrious predecessors, or, for that matter, in the work of his contemporaries. Not that he avoided making personal contacts. He was by no means devoid of social graces, but one wonders whether he ever experienced the feeling of genuine, sincere friendship, for he never showed very much desire for intimate personal confidences or for any of those moments of abandon which reveal the qualities and defects of the soul. He was too proud, too withdrawn, too jealous of his independence to trust anyone completely. As for his ever having been in love, we have no proof, no knowledge of any wife, mistress or even casual affair. 'He flirted with the wives of all his friends', says Anatole Jakovsky. But he gave no cause for umbrage, because nothing ever went beyond the very early stages. His love-life seems to have meant nothing more than an

198 Mondrian holding his painting *Composition in a Square with Red* 1943

occasional passing fancy. Van Gogh's failures with the opposite sex are easily explained by his unprepossessing appearance, his disconcerting stare, his churlish and often eccentric manners. Mondrian had none of these failings.

The truth of the matter is that never was any artist's existence so jealously, so fiercely protected against the intrusion of reality. His studio was like the cell of one of those learned Bollandists whose egotistical concentration on their chosen task prevented them from hearing life knocking on their door. Given over, body and soul, to his self-imposed assignment, Mondrian's sole passion was to see it through to the

199
Composition with Red (unfinished)
1938–44

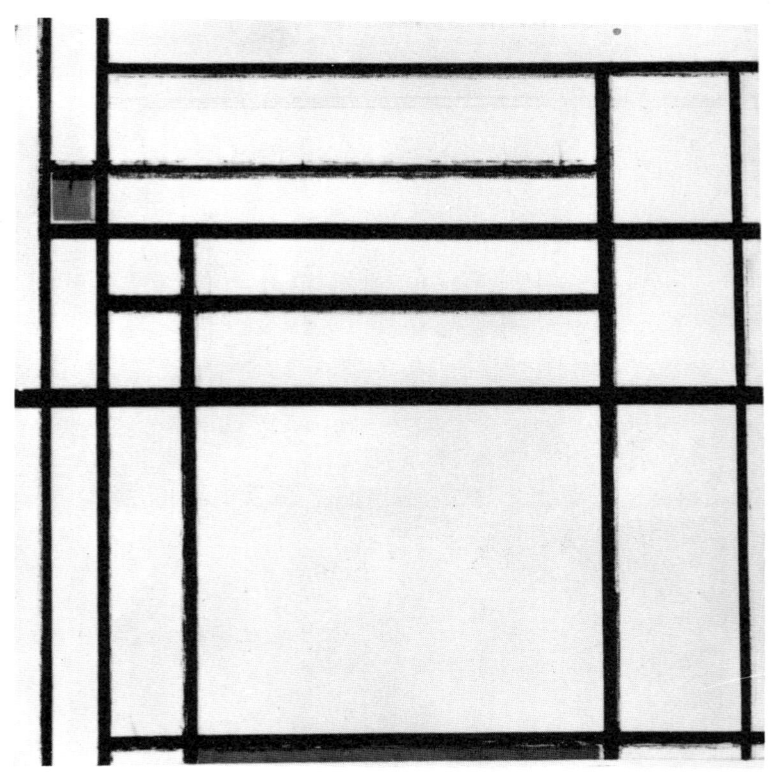

200 *Composition* (unfinished) 1939–44

end. It was the passion of a cenobite, an ascetic who does not wish to be disturbed by anyone or anything, a passion for what Plotinus called 'the most important'. It was a passion which could not allow the temporal to interfere with his search for the intemporal, for which he sacrificed his right to human happiness. But was he, after all, *un*-happy? He may have been denied the pleasures of the senses and the joys of shared affection, but, to make up for them, he experienced the exhilaration that comes from speculative thought and from spiritual certitude. Jos de Gruyter called him 'the Hegel of painting'.

201 *Composition with Red, Yellow and Blue* (unfinished) 1939–44

THE GRAND DESIGN

Everything points to the fact that Mondrian was not an artist by the grace of God, but that he conquered his genius by sheer will-power, perseverance and hard work, and that nothing, pleasure, women, honours or wealth, diverted him from his design – to transcend the individual in order to attain the universal, to approach as close as possible to perfection by discovering among the profusion of rhythms the

202 *Composition. London* 1940–2

one through which Being projects itself and affirms itself in its essence, and, from a state of everlasting flux, to extract original and immaculate truth. Such was the ruling passion of a man devoid of passions. Such was the ideal of a painter whose terrible lucidity was to isolate him from the common run of men.

Mondrian was fully aware of the fact that, although he was breaking new ground, he was also leading art into a blind alley. He was the end as well as the beginning. To go further than Mondrian towards absolute abstraction is impossible. His work is a challenge which it was beyond the powers of any one of his successors to accept, for, as he himself declared, his work marks 'the end of painting'. For him there was no question of being satisfied with playing aesthetic games or solving the kind of minor mathematical problems which had delighted countless artists in the past and continue to do so in the present. There must be no question of seeing in his pictures just a pleasing composition, an entertaining collection of geometrical figures arranged with a certain amount of ingenuity and taste. Art for art's sake was the least of Mondrian's concerns. His ambition was to express not life itself, but a rational and universal philosophy of life.

Until 1908, Mondrian's canvases were those of a not too gifted painter subject to the naturalism traditionally favoured in his country of origin. They in no way foreshadow the providential creator who was one day to revolutionize the fundamental laws of painting. Later, a sudden blaze of lyricism gives animation to his pictures. His touch is lighter, his colour brighter, richer and, on occasion, quite as violent as
Ills 37–40 that of the French fauves. In 1909 he started his series of *Trees* in which his art, shortly to be influenced by cubism, moved gradually from the figurative to the non-figurative. In 1918 he showed a completely new face. He began to speak a

203 *Composition with Red, Yellow and Blue* (unfinished) 1939–44

language hitherto unheard, stating and applying the principles and the rules of his doctrine of neo-plasticism. From then his works, without exception, were subject to the vertical-horizontal system, and his palette reduced to the three primary colours and the three 'non-colours', black, white and grey.

In his book *The Painter's Secret Geometry* (1963) Charles Bouleau, studying the formulas which, through the centuries, have governed the internal construction of works of art, claims to demonstrate that, in establishing his compositions on an architecture rigorous in plan, this 'cold, ruthless

204 *New York City I* 1941–2

Dutchman' was following the strict rule of the Golden Section. It is indeed possible that, although aiming at the expression of the constants of the human spirit, Mondrian might by chance have stumbled on 'divine proportion'. Nevertheless, I very much doubt that he did so intentionally,

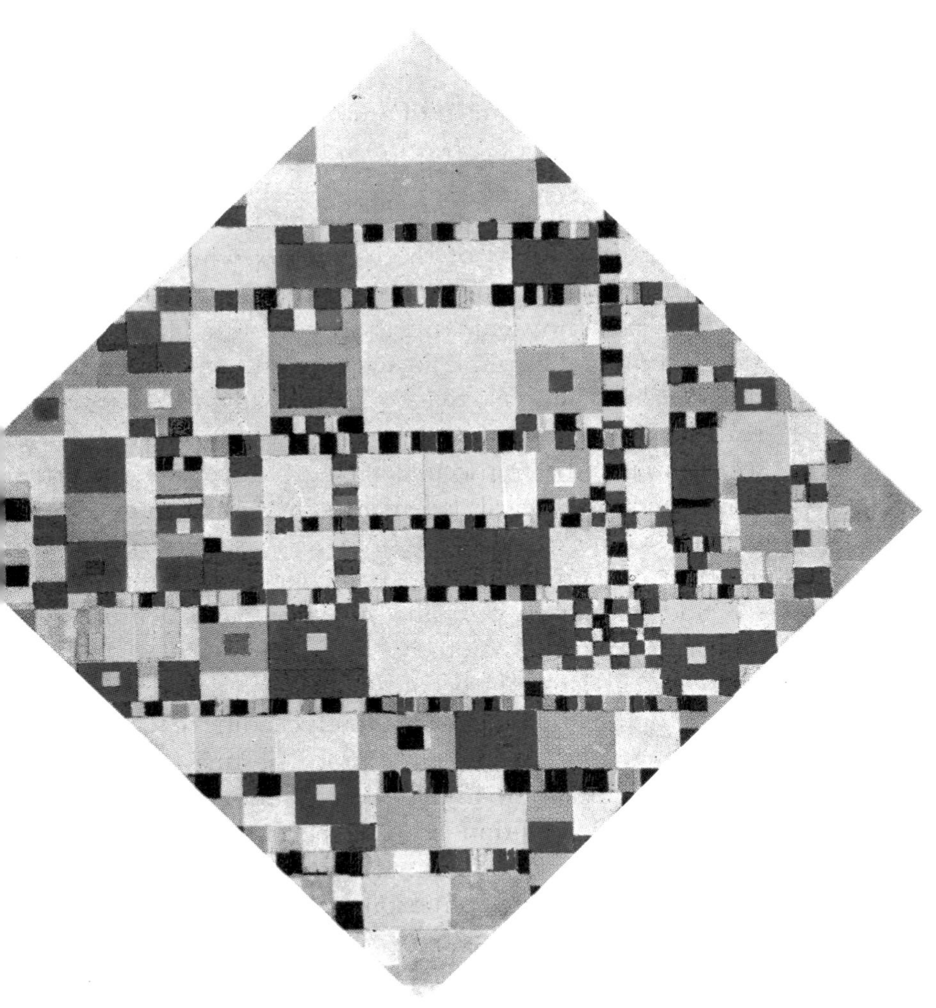

205 *Victory Boogie-Woogie* 1943–4

particularly as he made a point of breaking the relations between lines, planes and colours by graphic syncopation and discord. But when Charles Bouleau writes: 'Alberti's architectural plans had given artistic directives and criteria of beauty to the painters of his time, and Mondrian's pictures give to the architects of today guidance in the organization of their façades', who can refuse to agree with him? I would even go so far as to say that Mondrian's archetypes not only serve as a guide to architects, they also govern the geometrical creations of those painters who are the latest stalwarts of contemporary optical and visual art.

Mondrian is now enjoying a second youth. He is, for many artists, a unique example of tenacity and energy. We must not overlook the fact that, once he had moved from the realistic and analytical representation of nature to pure abstraction, a kind of transcendental logic urged him still further along the road towards laconicism. Once he had discovered the bases of his expressive system, he was not satisfied. For, if a fruit contains a stone, a stone contains all fruits. And so we find Mondrian pursuing his spiritual adventure with implacable determination.

We find his language becoming more and more simplified, more and more refined, as he himself becomes ever more and more exigent, more austere, more obstinately intent on attaining the Platonic ideal and, even though it may mean its being frozen within its own perfection, on achieving permanent beauty, total, timeless, absolute beauty. While he never repudiated his missionary past, he did, in his later years in New York, his only really happy years, belatedly cast aside his intransigence when he painted his *Boogie-Woogie* series, which is so exuberantly dynamic, but which he was prevented from completing. His best work was produced between 1921 and 1940, although we must not accept without reserves this two-dimensional art which is more graphic than plastic and more like a drawing by an architect than a picture by a painter.

In order to sift it even more, to concentrate and reduce it to bare essentials, until he was able at last to find those ideal

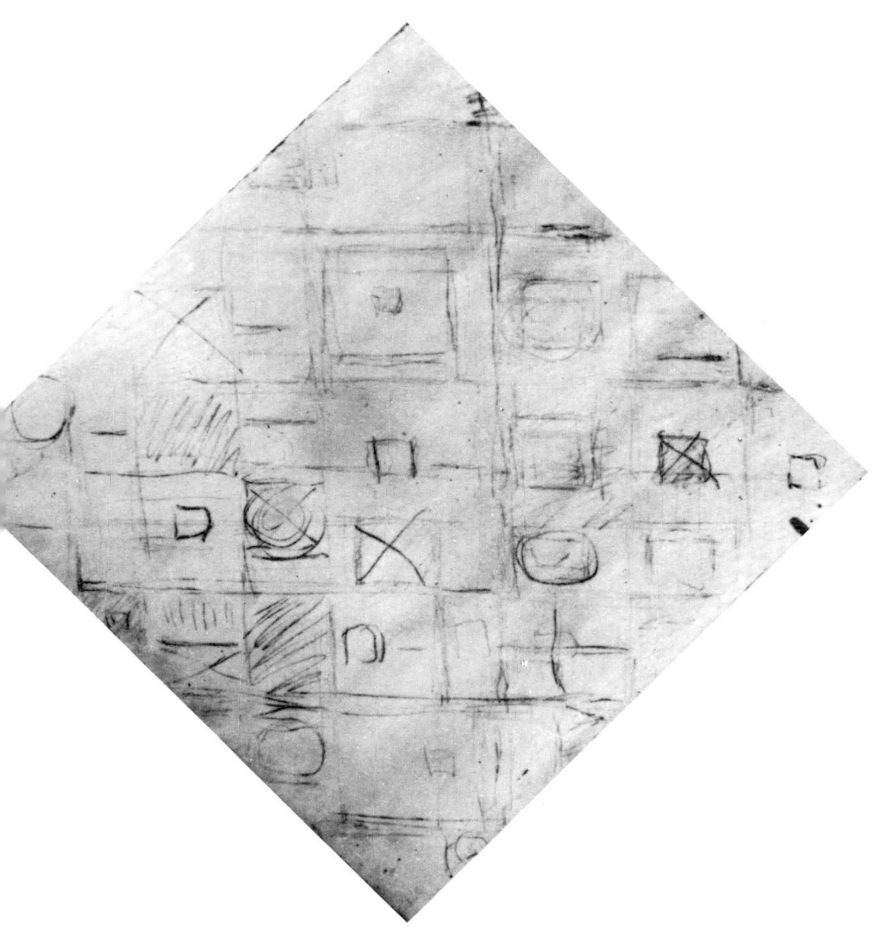

206 *Victory Boogie-Woogie* c. 1943

mathematical proportions and that supreme equilibrium beyond which lies the domain forbidden to the human will, he was not afraid to eliminate colour and to draw no more than two or three black lines on a light ground, as if his ultimate design had been to attain the white uniformity of the canvas, in other words, absolute negation, nothingness, the void. 'Piet Mondrian? No, *Niet* Mondrian!' was Salvador Dali's comment. Yet it is in the starkest of his works, in the extreme

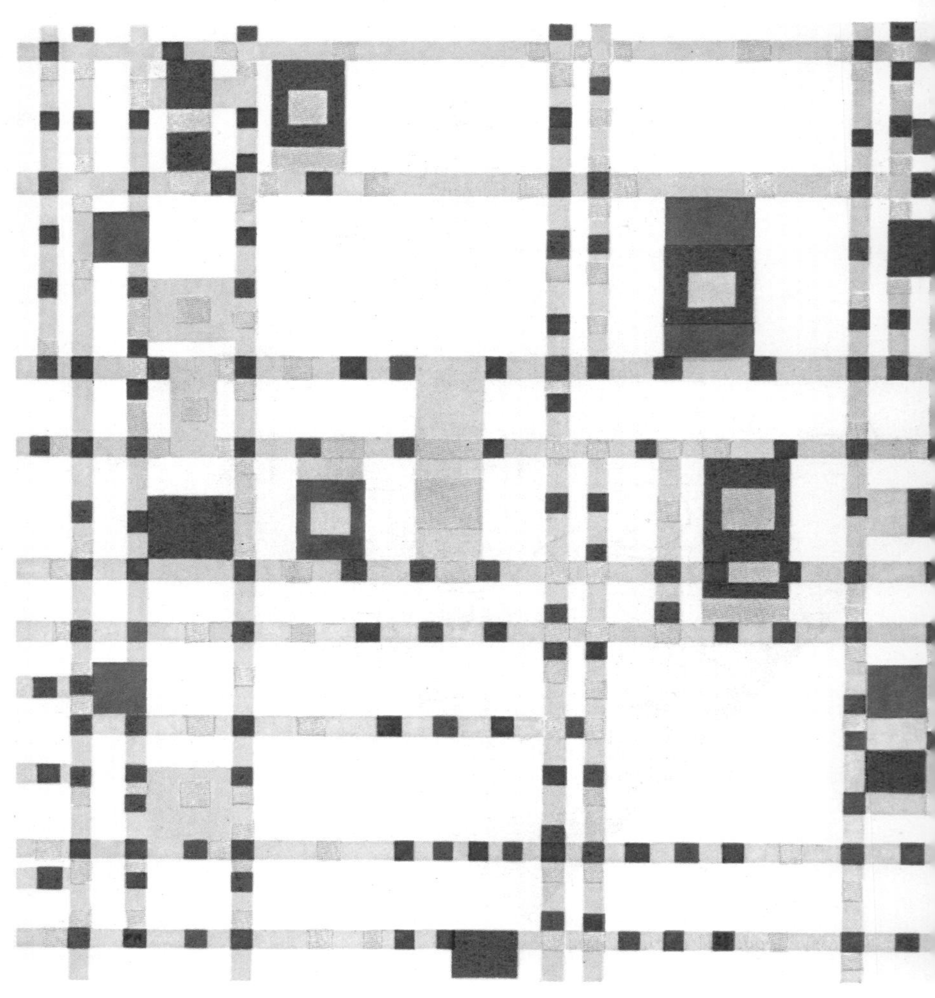

207 *Broadway Boogie-Woogie* 1942–3

tension between two straight lines, between pictorial space and natural space, that the full extent of his power is revealed. Where ordinary people would be able to see nothing, he was able to see the infinite struggle between cosmic forces. Instead of enriching mean subjects, he applied himself to limiting a field of inspiration that was too vast, and to impoverishing a theme that was too rich. And when, proud of his achievement, he should have stopped at that, he had the audacity to go still further. Far from squandering the superabundance of his inner energy, he used it to assuage his hunger for purity, the kind of purity that is often confused with poverty, and by doing so he crystalized into a definitive paradigm the shifting powers which are hidden from us by appearances. It is, however, when his composition is at its

208 *Broadway Boogie-Woogie* Study 1942

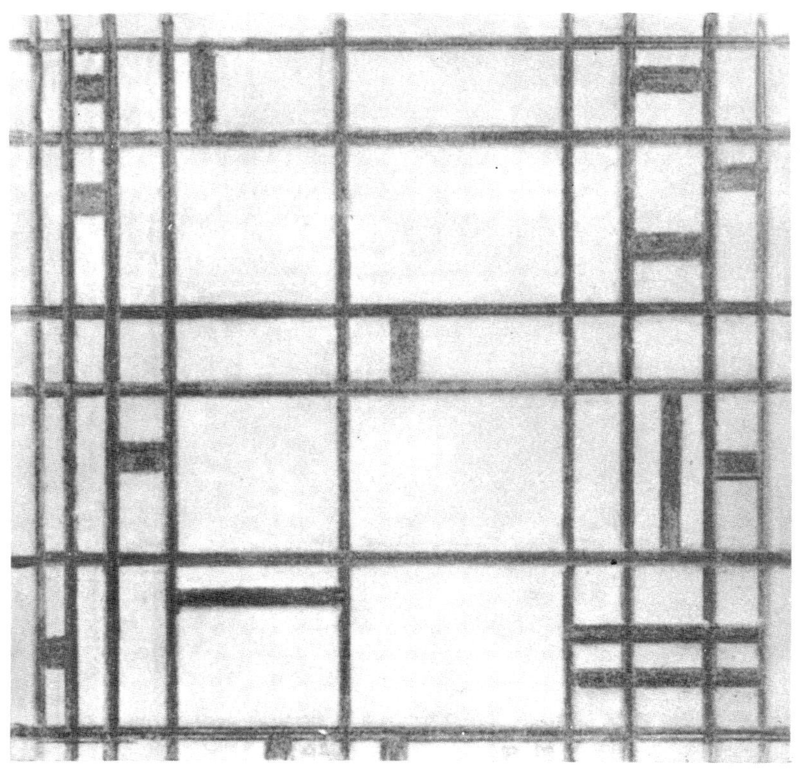

most sober that it is least open to criticism, for then it is the image of pure rhythm, of sovereign proportion, of perfect harmony, an image that looks cold, inhuman, frigid. But within it pulses an invisible spark, whereas unrestrained lyricism, unbridled passion and uncontrolled fantasies often conceal nothing but dead ashes.

Had Mondrian left only a score of canvases of such conciseness, they would have been amply sufficient to establish his greatness. So long as one looks at them without prejudice, one can see in them the Idea made Sensation and be fascinated by their stony silence, their diamond-hard light, their remote, invulnerable serenity, withdrawn beyond the passage of time, and by their world of evidence and intelligibility in which our aspirations to eternity find refuge. They remind one inevitably of those pyramids, temples and tombs of Antiquity, subject to the science of numbers and the rigid ordering of surfaces, and of the ancient civilizations which, to ensure the survival of their monuments, built them with simple blocks of stone hewn and assembled according to the laws of geometry and equilibrium. They remind one, too, of those architect-theologians who, in their grandiose structures, represented divine wisdom, the permanence of the sacred and the symbol of the cosmos.

Such is the work of Mondrian. In it, as in those ancient monuments, with their stable, logical, incorruptible order and that construction of the mind which spurns the contingent, the accidental, the fortuitous, there is no room for pretence and trickery. It is the art of a man devoid of sensuality, a rationalist with a background of mysticism, a man whose audacity was based on reflection, whose intense integrity made him a sectarian and whose reticence made him anti-romantic. It is the work of a creator who succeeded in arousing emotion by method, calculation and proportion.

Chronology
Select bibliography
List of illustrations
Acknowledgments
Index

Chronology

1872 March 7, born Amersfoort, Holland (Pieter Cornelis Mondriaan)
1880 Family moves to Winterswijk; brother, Carel, born there.
1889 Receives diploma for teaching in elementary schools.
1892 Receives diploma for teaching in secondary schools. However, refuses to take a teaching post and, against his father's wishes, enrols in the Amsterdam Academy of Fine Arts.
1901 Visits Spain with Simon Maris.
1903 Visits Brabant (Holland).
1904 January, moves to Uden (Brabant) where he remains for a year; inspired by Van Gogh.
1905 February, returns to Amsterdam.
1907 Summer with the painter Hulshoff at Oele (in the province of Overijssel). Paints undistinguished landscapes.
1908 Meets Jan Toorop during his first visit to Domburg, on the island of Walcheren. Radical change in painting style, 'Zeeland period' commences. Spends following four summers at Domburg.
1909 January, exhibits at the Stedelijk Museum, Amsterdam, with Jan Sluyters and Cornelis Spoor. His work is violently attacked by the critics. Beginning of greater interest in theosophy.
1910 May, exhibits at the Sint Lucas Gilde, Amsterdam, with the Luminists.
1911 Becomes member of board of directors of the Moderne Kunstkring. In December leaves for Paris, where Conrad Kickert lends him his studio at 26 Rue du Départ. Changes his name Mondriaan to Mondrian.
1912–13 Style of painting changes radically under Cubist influence. Begins to move towards 'pure abstraction'. Exhibits paintings at the Salon des Indépendents.
1914 Returns to Holland because of father's illness. While there, the war breaks out so he remains home until 1919.
1915 Father dies. Meets the painter Theo van Doesburg.
1916 Meets Van der Leck.
1917 Founding of *De Stijl* with Van Doesburg. First issue published October.
1919 February, returns to Paris.
1920 *Le Néo-Plasticisme* published in Paris by Léonce Rosenberg.
1923 November exhibition of De Stijl group at Léonce Rosenberg's.
1925 *Le Néo-Plasticisme* published in Germany by the Bauhaus under the title *Neue Gestaltung*.
1926 First exhibition in America at the Brooklyn Museum under the auspices of Katherine S. Dreier.

1929 Becomes member of the group Cercle et Carré; publishes in its review the article 'L'Art réaliste et l'art superréaliste'.

1932–8 Exhibits with Abstraction-Création group. Remains in Paris at 26 Rue du Départ until 1936, when he moves to Boulevard Raspail.

1938 September, leaves for London.

1940 October 3, arrives in New York, where he makes friends with other artists, many of whom are also European war refugees.

1942 January–February, first one-man exhibition at Valentin Dudensing's gallery in New York.

1943 Second exhibition at Dudensing's.

1944 February 1, dies at Murray Hill Hospital, New York, of pneumonia.

Select bibliography

WRITINGS BY MONDRIAN

'De Nieuwe Beelding in de schilderkunst', eleven instalments, *De Stijl*, 1917–18.

'Het bepaalde en het onbepaalde', *De Stijl*, 1918.

'Dialog over de Nieuwe Beelding', two instalments, *De Stijl*, 1919.

'Natuurlijke en abstracte realiteit', thirteen instalments, *De Stijl*, 1919–20.

'De groote boulevards', *De Nieuwe Amsterdammer*, 1920.

'Le Néo-plasticisme', *L'Effort Moderne*, Paris 1920.

'De Bruiteurs futuristes Italiens' en "het" nieuwe in de muziek', *De Stijl*, 1921.

'Het Néo-plasticisme (de Nieuwe Beelding) en zijn (Hare) realiseering in de muziek', *De Stijl*, 1922.

'De realiseering van het Néo-plasticisme in verre toekomst en in de huidige architectuur', *De Stijl*, 1922.

'Schilderkunst', *De Stijl*, 1922.

'La manifestation du néo-plasticisme dans la musique et les bruiteurs italiens', *La vie des lettres et des arts*, Paris 1922.

'Le néo-plasticisme, sa réalisation dans la musique et au théâtre futur', *La vie des lettres et des arts*, Paris 1922.

'Die neue Gestaltung in der Musik und die futuristischen italienischen Bruitisten', *De Stijl*, 1923.

'Moet de schilderkunst minderwaardig zijn aan de bouwkunst?', *De Stijl*, 1923.

'Les arts et la beauté de notre ambiance tangible', *Manomètre*, Lyons 1924.

'Geen Axioma maar beeldend principe', *De Stijl*, 1924.

'De huif naar den wind', *De Stijl*, 1924.

Die neue Gestaltung. Munich, Bauhausbücher, 1925.

'De jazz en de neo-plastiek', *International Revue*, I 10, Amsterdam, 1927.

'Néo-plasticisme', *International Revue*, I 10, Amsterdam 1927.

'Ne pas s'occuper de la forme. . .' *Cercle et Carré*, No. 1, Paris 1930.

'L'Art réaliste et l'Art Superréaliste (la Morphoplastique et la néoplastique)', *Cercle et Carré*, No. 2, Paris 1930.

'De l'art abstrait. Réponse de Piet Mondrian', *Cahiers d'art*, Paris 1931. English translation in *Art Students League Quarterly*, No. 1, Spring, 1941.

Note by P.M. in the last number of *De Stijl*, January 1932.

Notes by P.M. in the albums of the Abstraction-Creation group, No. 1 (1932), No. 2 (1933), No. 3 (1934).

'Plastic Art and Pure Plastic Art', *Circle*, London 1937.

Kunst zonder onderwerp. Amsterdam, Stedelijk Museum, 1938.

Toward the True Vision of Reality.

New York, Valentine Gallery, 1942.

Pure Plastic Art. (For Helena Rubinstein Salon.) New York, New York Art Center, 1942.

'Abstract Art', Preface to *Art of this Century*, New York 1942.

Plastic Art and Pure Plastic Art and other essays. Six Mondrian essays in English. New York, Wittenborn, 1945. (Third edition, 1951.)

A New Realism, New York 1946.

Pure beelding. Amsterdam, Stedelijk Museum, 1946.

Lebenserinnerungen und Gedanken über die Neue Gestaltung.

'La vraie valeur des oppositions', *Cahiers d'art*, Paris 1947.

'L'expression plastique nouvelle dans la peinture', *Cahiers d'art*, Paris 1947. (The article had originally appeared in the first issue of this periodical.)

'El neo-plasticismo', fragments, *Ciclo*, Buenos-Aires 1949.

'Le Home – la rue – la cité', excerpts in *Art d'Aujourd'hui*, Paris, December 1949.

'Home – Street – City', *Transformation*, No. 1, New York 1950.

In Our Time. . . (partial translation of an article which appeared in *Cahiers d'Art* in 1931.) New York, Sidney Janis Gallery, 1951.

'Extraits de lettres à Théo van Doesburg', Catalogue of the *De Stijl* Exhibition, Stedelijk Museum, Amsterdam 1951.

'New Art – New Life', *De Stijl, 1917–1931.* Amsterdam, Meulenhoff, 1956.

BIOGRAPHY AND CRITICISM

JOOST BALJEU *Theo van Doesburg and De Stijl* (to be published shortly via the Rijksbureau voor Kunsthistorische Documentatie, The Hague).

CORNELIS BLOK *Mondriaan in de collectie van het Haags Gemeentemuseum catalogus 1964*, The Hague, Gemeentemuseum, 1964.

ALBERTO BUSIGNANI *Mondrian*, London, Thames and Hudson, New York, Grosset and Dunlap, 1968 (original Italian edition Florence, Sadea/Sansoni 1968).

ROBERT L. HERBERT *Modern Artists on Art*, New York 1964.

SAM HUNTER *Mondrian*, New York, Abrams, 1958.

H. L. C. JAFFÉ *Inleiding tot de Kunst van Mondriaan*, Assen/Amsterdam, Born, 1959.

H. L. C. JAFFÉ *De Stijl 1917–1931: Dutch Contribution to Modern Art*, London, Alec Tiranti, 1956.

H. L. C. JAFFÉ *The 'De Stijl' Group*, Amsterdam, J. M. Melehoff, 1964 (?) (adapted from Dortmund Catalogue 1964).

H. L. C. JAFFÉ *De Stijl*, London, Thames and Hudson, New York, McGraw-Hill, 1968 (original German edition, Cologne, DuMont-Schauberg, 1967).

DAVID LEWIS *Mondrian*, New York, Wittenborn, 1957.

A. B. LOOSJES-TERPSTRA *Moderne Kunst in Nederland 1900–1914*, Utrecht, Haentjens Dekker and Gumbert, 1959.

F. M. LURASCO *Onze Modern Meesters*, Amsterdam, C. L. G. Veldt, 1907.

FILIBERTO MENNA *Mondrian: Cultura e Poesia*, Rome, Edizioni dell'Ateneo, 1962.

OTTAVIO MORISANI *L'Astrattismo di Piet Mondrian*, Venice, Neri Pozza Editore, 1956.

CARLO RAGGHIANTI *Mondrian e l'Arte del XX secolo*, Milan, Edizioni di Comunita, 1962.

MICHEL SEUPHOR *Piet Mondrian: Life and Work*, London, Thames and

Hudson, New York, Abrams, 1956 (original French edition Paris, Flammarion).

L. J. F. WIJSENBEEK and J. J. P. OUD *Mondriaan*, Zeist (The Netherlands), W. de Haan, 1962.

ARTICLES

JOOST BALJEU 'The Problem of Reality with Suprematism, Constructivism, Proun, Neoplasticism and Elementarism', *The Lugano Review* 1: no. 1, 1965, pp. 105–24.

ALFRED H. BARR *De Stijl* 1917–28, New York, Museum of Modern Art, 1961.

CORNELIS BLOK 'Mondriaan's Vroege Werk', *Museumjournaal voor Modern Kunst*, August 1962, Series 8, no. 2, pp. 33–41 (resumé in French, p. 46).

MARTIN S. JAMES 'The Realism Behind Mondrian's Geometry', *Art News LVI* (December 1957), pp. 34–7.

MARTIN S. JAMES 'Mondrian and the Dutch Symbolists', *The Art Journal* XXIII, no. 2 (1963–4), pp. 103–11.

J. J. SWEENEY Piet Mondrian, New York Museum of Modern Art, 1948 (reprinted from *M.M.A. Bulletin*, vol. XII, no. 4, and *M.M.A. Bulletin*, vol. XIII, nos. 4–5).

MICHEL SEUPHOR 'Piet Mondrian 1914–18', *Magazine of Art* XLV, no. 5 (1952), pp. 216–23.

CHARMION VON WIEGAND 'The Meaning of Mondrian', *Journal of Aesthetics* II, no. 8 (fall 1943), pp. 62–70.

List of illustrations

The French titles and the catalogue numbers are taken from the classified catalogue contained in Michel Seuphor's *Piet Mondrian: Life and Work* (see Bibliography).

1 *Self-portrait c.* 1900
(Portrait du peintre par lui-même)
oil on canvas
49×38 cm.
Phillips Gallery, Washington
cat. 1

2 *Church Apse c.* 1892
(Abside d'église)
oil on canvas
60×49 cm.
J. P. Smid, Amsterdam

3 *Herrings and Lemons* 1893
(Nature morte aux poissons)
oil on canvas
66×74 cm.
Stedelijk Museum, Amsterdam
cat. 30

4 *Landscape with Houses and Canal c.* 1897
(Paysage avec maisons et canal)
oil on canvas
34×52 cm.
Monet Art Gallery, Amsterdam

5 *Spring Idyll* 1900
(Idylle printanière)
oil on canvas
75×64 cm.
Mrs I. J. Bantzinger-Wiedenhoff, Amsterdam
cat. 12

6 *Factory* 1899
crayon drawing
19×27 cm.
J. P. Smid, Amsterdam

7 *Mill by the Water c.* 1900
(Moulin au bord de l'eau)
oil on canvas
30×37.5 cm.
The Museum of Modern Art, New York
cat. 105

8 *Autumn Landscape c.* 1902
(Paysage d'automne)
drawing
33×41 cm.
S. B. Slijper, Blaricum
cat. 77

9 *Woods near Oele c.* 1907
(Bois près d'Oele)
drawing
111×67 cm.
S. B. Slijper, Blaricum
cat. 64

10 *Landscape* 1907
(Paysage au clair de lune)
oil on canvas
71×112 cm.
Stedelijk Museum, Amsterdam
cat. 50

11 *Sketch for Landscape near Oele* c. 1907
(Esquisse pour Paysage près d'Oele)
charcoal drawing
28.7 × 31.2 cm.
Gemeentemuseum, The Hague
cat. 48

12 *Evening Sky* 1907–8
(Ciel au crépuscule)
oil on canvas
64 × 74 cm.
Monet Art Gallery, Amsterdam

13 *Trees on the Banks of the Gein at Moonrise* 1907–8
(Esquisse pour Près du Gein: Arbres avec lune montante)
charcoal drawing
63 × 75 cm.
S. B. Slijper, Blaricum
cat. 71

14 *Trees on the Banks of the Gein at Moonrise* 1907–8
(Près du Gein: Arbres avec lune montante)
oil on canvas
79 × 92.5 cm.
Gemeentemuseum, The Hague
cat. 72

15 *The Amstel River, Evening Impression* 1907
charcoal drawing
34 × 49.3 cm.
Gemeentemuseum, The Hague
On loan from S. B. Slijper

16 *The River Amstel in the Evening* c. 1907
drawing
Frans Hals Museum, Haarlem

17 *Farm at Duivendrecht* before 1908
(Ferme à Duivendrecht)
watercolour
49 × 64 cm.
Frans Hals Museum, Haarlem
cat. 118

18 *Farm at Duivendrecht* c. 1908
(Ferme à Duivendrecht)
oil on canvas
85.5 × 108.5 cm.
Gemeentemuseum, The Hague
On loan from S. B. Slijper
cat. 120

19 *Chrysanthemums* c. 1908–10
(Chrysanthèmes)
oil on canvas
45.5 × 33 cm.
S. B. Slijper, Blaricum
cat. 139

20 *Dying Chrysanthemum* c. 1907
(Chrysanthème mourant) (esquisse)
charcoal drawing
78 × 46 cm.
S. B. Slijper, Blaricum
cat. 135

21 *Dying Chrysanthemum* 1908
(Chrysanthème mourant)
oil on canvas
84.5 × 54 cm.
Gemeentemuseum, The Hague
On loan from S. B. Slijper
cat. 136

22 *Dying Sunflower* 1907–8
(Soleil mourant)
oil on canvas
65 × 34 cm.
Gemeentemuseum, The Hague
On loan from S. B. Slijper
cat. 155

23 *Tiger Lily* 1909
watercolour
39 × 44 cm.
Mrs A. C. H. W. Smid-Verlee, Amsterdam

24 *Hayricks c.* 1909
(Meules)
oil on canvas
30×43 cm.
Mrs Maria Johanna Ootmar,
Kelowna, British Columbia
cat. 168

25 *The Red Cloud* 1907
oil on canvas
64×75 cm.
Gemeentemuseum, The Hague

26 *Woods near Oele* 1908
(Bois près d'Oele)
oil on canvas
128×158 cm.
Gemeentemuseum, The Hague
On loan from S. B. Slijper
cat. 65

27 *Lighthouse at Westkapelle* 1910
(Tour-phare à Westkapelle)
oil on canvas
39×29.5 cm.
Gemeentemuseum, The Hague
On loan from S. B. Slijper
cat. 244

28 *Windmill in Sunlight c.* 1911
(Moulin au soleil)
oil on canvas
114×87 cm.
Gemeentemuseum, The Hague
On loan from S. B. Slijper
cat. 113

29 *Church Tower in Zouteland* 1910
Tour de l'église (à Zoutelande
sur Walcheren)
oil on canvas
89.5×61.5 cm.
M. J. Heybroek, Hilversum
cat. 247

30 *The Red Mill* 1910–11
(Moulin à Domberg)
oil on canvas
150×86 cm.
Gemeentemuseum, The Hague
On loan from S. B. Slijper
cat. 112

31 *Church Tower at Domburg*
1910–11
(Tour de l'église de Domburg)
oil on canvas
114×75 cm.
Gemeentemuseum, The Hague
On loan from S. B. Slijper
cat. 251

32 *The Red Tree* 1909–10
(L'arbre rouge)
oil on canvas
70×99 cm.
Gemeentemuseum, The Hague
cat. 171

33 *Dune c.* 1910
(Dune)
oil on canvas
36×41 cm.
S. B. Slijper, Blaricum
cat. 218

34 *Dune c.* 1910
(Dune)
oil on canvas
33×43 cm.
G. J. Nieuwenhuizen Segaar
Gallery, The Hague
cat. 212

35 *Dunes and Sea* 1909
(Dunes et mer)
pencil drawing
10×17 cm.
Harry Holtzman, New York
cat. 205

36 *Dune V* 1909–10
(Dune)
oil on canvas
65.5×96 cm.
Gemeentemuseum, The Hague
cat. 214

37 *Tree c.* 1909–10
(Arbre)
chalk drawing
32×49 cm.
M. J. Heybroek, Hilversum
cat. 170

38 *Trees c.* 1911
(Arbres)
charcoal drawing
17.5×12.5 cm.
Harry Holtzman, New York
cat. 185

39 *Tree c.* 1911
(Arbre)
charcoal drawing
Harry Holtzman, New York
cat. 187

40 *Tree c.* 1911
(Arbre)
charcoal drawing
12.5×18 cm.
Harry Holtzman, New York
cat. 188

41 *The Grey Tree* 1912
(L'arbre argenté)
oil on canvas
78.5×107.5 cm.
Gemeentemuseum, The Hague
On loan from S. B. Slijper
cat. 177

42 *Tree* 1911
(Arbre)
oil on canvas
76×102 cm.
Munson Williams Proctor
Institute, U.S.A.
cat. 176

43 *Composition with Trees* 1912
(Composition avec arbres)
oil on canvas
81×62 cm.
Gemeentemuseum, The Hague
On loan from S. B. Slijper
cat. 195

44 *Tree* 1912
(Arbre)
oil on canvas
92.5×70 cm.
Museum of Art, Carnegie
Institute, Pittsburg
cat. 192

45 Mondrian's Studio,
26 Rue du Départ, Paris

46 *Self-portrait* 1911
(Portrait du peintre par lui-
même)
charcoal drawing
Gemeentemuseum, The Hague
On loan from S. B. Slijper
cat. 5

47 *Nude Study* 1912
(Nu)
charcoal drawing
92.5×158 cm.
Harry Holtzman, New York
cat. 29

48 *Sunflowers* 1912–13
charcoal drawing
30.5×24.4 cm.
J. P. Smid, Amsterdam

49 *Female Nude c.* 1912
(Nu)
oil on canvas
140×78 cm.
Gemeentemuseum, The Hague
On loan from S. B. Slijper
cat. 28

50 *Composition No. 1 (Trees)* 1912
(Composition No. 1) (Arbres)
oil on canvas
87.5×75.4 cm.
J. Hudig L. Izn, Rotterdam
cat. 193

51 *Oval Composition, Sketch* 1913
(Composition ovale) (esquisse)
charcoal drawing
85×70 cm.

Gemeentemuseum, The Hague
On loan from S. B. Slijper
cat. 199

52 *Still Life with Ginger Pot I* 1911
(Nature morte au pot de gingembre I)
oil on canvas
65.5×75 cm.
Gemeentemuseum, The Hague
On loan from S. B. Slijper
cat. 33

53 *Still Life with Ginger Pot II* 1912
(Nature morte au pot de gingembre II)
oil on canvas
92×105 cm.
Gemeentemuseum, The Hague
On loan from S. B. Slijper
cat. 34

54 *Composition No. 7* 1913
oil on canvas
102×112 cm.
Solomon R. Guggenheim Museum, New York
cat. 265

55 *Composition No. 11 c.* 1912
oil on canvas
76×57.5 cm.
Rijksmuseum Kröller-Müller, Otterlo
cat. 19

56 *Oval Composition (Trees)* 1913
(Composition ovale) (Arbres)
oil on canvas
94×78 cm.
Stedelijk Museum, Amsterdam
cat. 200

57 *Tableau I* 1913
oil on canvas
96×64 cm.
Rijksmuseum Kröller-Müller, Otterlo
cat. 266

58 *Scaffolding c.* 1912
(Echafaudage)
charcoal drawing
153×112 cm.
Peggy Guggenheim Collection, Venice
cat. 277

59 *Oval Composition (Sketch)* 1912
(Composition ovale) (Esquisse)
charcoal drawing
103.5×64 cm.
Harry Holtzman, New York
cat. 282

60 *Composition in Blue, Grey and Pink* 1913
(Composition en bleu, gris et rose)
oil on canvas
88×115 cm.
Rijksmuseum Kröller-Müller, Otterlo
cat. 270

61 *Façade No. 7* 1914
oil on canvas
56×84 cm.
Sidney Janis Gallery, New York
cat. 272

62 *Composition in Grey and Yellow* 1914
(Composition en gris et jaune)
oil on canvas
61.5×75.5 cm.
Stedelijk Museum, Amsterdam
cat. 269

63 *Façade in Brown and Grey* 1913
(Façade en brun et gris)
oil on canvas
63.5×91 cm.
Edgar Kaufmann, New York
cat. 267

64 *Church Façade* 1914
(Façade d'église)
charcoal drawing

Private collection
cat. 257

65 *Church at Domburg* 1914
(Église à Domburg)
India ink
63 × 50 cm.
Gemeentemuseum, The Hague
On loan from S. B. Slijper
cat. 254

66 *The Sea c.* 1914
(La mer)
pencil drawing
10 × 17 cm.
Harry Holtzman, New York
cat. 224

67 *The Sea* 1913–14
(La mer)
gouache and India ink
50 × 61 cm.
Harry Holtzman, New York
cat. 277

68 *The Sea* 1914
(La mer)
charcoal drawing
95 × 128 cm.
Peggy Guggenheim Collection, Venice
cat. 229

69 *The Sea c.* 1914
(La mer)
charcoal drawing
48 × 61 cm.
Théodore Bally, Montreux
cat. 228

70 *Composition with Colour Planes* 1914
(Composition avec plans de couleur)
oil on canvas
Sidney Janis Gallery, New York
cat. 284

71 *Composition No. 9. Scaffolding* *c.* 1913
(Composition No. 9)
(Echafaudage)
oil on canvas
95.2 × 67.5 cm.
The Museum of Modern Art, New York
Gift Mr and Mrs Armand P. Bartos
cat. 279

72 *Pier and Ocean* 1914
(Jetée et Océan)
charcoal drawing
57 × 63 cm.
Gemeentemuseum, The Hague
On loan from S. B. Slijper
cat. 237

73 *Pier and Ocean* 1914
(Jetée et Océan)
tempera and India ink
50.2 × 63 cm.
Burton Tremaine, Meriden, Conn.
cat. 235

74 *Pier and Ocean* 1915
(Jetée et Océan)
oil on canvas
85 × 105 cm.
Rijksmuseum Kröller-Müller, Otterlo
cat. 239

75 *Oval Composition with Bright Colours* 1913
(Composition ovale avec couleurs claires)
oil on canvas
107 × 79 cm.
The Museum of Modern Art, New York
cat. 283

76 *Composition No. 6* 1914
88 × 61 cm.
Gemeentemuseum, The Hague
On loan from S. B. Slijper
cat. 273

77 *Composition c.* 1916
oil on canvas
124.5 × 75 cm.
Harry Holtzman, New York
cat. 231

78 *Composition with Lines* 1917
(Composition avec lignes)
oil on canvas
108.4 × 108.4 cm.
Rijksmuseum Kröller-Müller, Otterlo
cat. 233

79 *Oval Composition* 1913–14
(Composition ovale)
oil on canvas
113 × 84.5 cm.
Gemeentemuseum, The Hague
On loan from S. B. Slijper
cat. 281

80 *Composition* 1916
oil on canvas
120 × 75 cm.
Solomon R. Guggenheim Museum, New York
cat. 232

81 Bart van der Leck:
Geometric Composition No. 1 1917
oil on canvas
95 × 102 cm.
Rijksmuseum Kröller-Müller, Otterlo

82 Bart van der Leck:
Geometric Composition No. 2 1917
oil on canvas
94 × 100 cm.
Rijksmuseum Kröller-Müller

83 *Composition in Blue B* 1917
(Composition en bleu, B)
oil on canvas
50 × 48 cm.
Rijksmuseum Kröller-Müller, Otterlo
cat. 291

84 *Composition No. 3 with Colour Planes* 1917
(Composition No. 3 avec plans de couleur)
oil on canvas
48 × 61 cm.
Gemeentemuseum, The Hague
cat. 286

85 *Composition with Colour Planes B* 1917
(Composition avec plans de couleur B)
oil on canvas
44 × 50 cm.
Rijksmuseum Kröller-Müller, Otterlo
cat. 285

86 *Composition with Colour Planes on White Ground A* 1917
(Composition aux plans de couleurs pure sur fond blanc A)
oil on canvas
50 × 45 cm.
Rijksmuseum Kröller-Müller, Otterlo
cat. 290

87 *Composition. Colour Planes with Grey Contours* 1918
(Composition: Plans de couleur avec lignes grises)
oil on canvas
49 × 60.5 cm.
Max Bill, Zurich and Ulm
cat. 301

88 Theo van Doesburg:
Contre Composition 1924
100 × 100 cm.
Stedelijk Museum, Amsterdam

89 Vilmos Huszar:
Composition 1916
Design for *De Stijl* cover
60 × 50 cm.
Rijks Verspreide Kunstvoorwerpen, The Hague

90 *Composition: Lozenge with Grey Lines* 1918
(Composition dans le carreau avec lignes grises)
oil on canvas
diagonal 121 cm.
Gemeentemuseum, The Hague
cat. 297

91 *Lozenge Composition* 1919
(Composition dans le carreau)
oil on canvas
49×49 cm.
Rijksmuseum Kröller-Müller, Otterlo
cat. 300

92 *Composition in Grey and Light Brown* 1918
(Composition en gris et ocre-brun)
oil on canvas
80×50 cm.
The Museum of Fine Arts, Houston
Gift of Mr and Mrs Pierre Schlumberger
cat. 294

93 *Composition* 1919
oil on canvas
79×79 cm.
Sidney Janis Gallery, New York
cat. 302

94 Theo van Doesburg. Decoration for the Café Aubette in Strasbourg 1926–27
From *Encyclopaedia of Modern Architecture*, London, Thames and Hudson, 1963

95 *Self-portrait c.* 1918 (signed 1916)
(Portrait du peintre par lui-même)
charcoal drawing
121×63 cm.
Gemeentemuseum, The Hague
On loan from S. B. Slijper

96 *Composition with Red, Blue, Black and Yellow-Green* 1920
(Composition avec rouge, bleu, noir et jaune-vert)
oil on canvas
80×80 cm.
The Museum of Modern Art, New York
cat. 305

97 *Composition in Grey, Red, Yellow and Blue* 1920
(Composition en gris, rouge, jaune et bleu)
oil on canvas
100.5×101 cm.
The Museum of Modern Art, New York
On loan from Mr Harry Holtzman
cat. 303

98 *Composition. Checkerboard, Dark Colours* 1919
(Composition dans le damier aux couleurs sombres)
oil on canvas
84×102 cm.
Gemeentemuseum, The Hague
On loan from S. B. Slijper
cat. 293

99 *Composition. Checkerboard, Bright Colours* 1919
(Composition dans le damier aux couleurs claires)
oil on canvas
86×106 cm.
Gemeentemuseum, The Hague
On loan from S. B. Slijper
cat. 292

100 *Composition* 1921
oil on canvas
49.5×45.5 cm.

Kunstmuseum, Basle
Emil Hoffman Fund
cat. 314

101 *Composition with Red, Yellow and Blue* 1921
(Composition avec rouge, jaune et bleu)
oil on canvas
39.5 × 35 cm.
Gemeentemuseum, The Hague
On loan from S. B. Slijper
cat. 321

102 *Composition. Bright Colour Planes with Grey Lines* 1919
(Composition de couleurs claires avec lignes grises)
oil on canvas
diagonal 84 cm.
Rijksmuseum Kröller-Müller, Otterlo
cat. 299

103 *Composition. Bright Colour Planes with Grey Lines* 1919
(Composition aux couleurs claires avec contours gris)
oil on canvas
49 × 49 cm.
Mrs Marguerite Hagenbach, Basle
cat. 296

104 *Composition with Large Blue Plane and Red and Yellow Rectangles* 1921
(Composition avec bleu étendu, rouge et jaune)
oil on canvas
Sidney Janis Gallery, New York
cat. 317

105 *Composition with Red, Blue and Yellow-Green* 1920
oil on canvas
67 × 57 cm.
Wilhelm Hack, Koeln-Bayenthal
cat. 306

106 *Composition in a Square* 1921
(Composition dans le carré)
oil on canvas
John L. Senior Jr., New York
cat. 400

107 *Tableau No. I* 1921–25
oil on canvas
75 × 65 cm.
Moser-Schindler, Zurich
cat. 307

108 *Composition* 1921
oil on canvas
99 × 100 cm.
Mr and Mrs Armand P. Bartos, New York
cat. 313

109 *Composition with Red, Yellow and Blue* 1921
(Composition avec rouge, jaune et bleu)
oil on canvas
103 × 100 cm.
Gemeentemuseum, The Hague
On loan from S. B. Slijper
cat. 315

110 *Composition* 1922
oil on canvas
Harry Holtzman, New York
cat. 327

111 *Composition c.* 1922
oil on canvas
80 × 50.7 cm.
Dr and Mrs Israel Rosen, Baltimore
cat. 320

112 *Composition in a Square with Red, Yellow and Blue c.* 1925
(Composition dans le carré avec rouge, jaune et bleu)
oil on canvas
Harry Holtzman, New York
cat. 401

113 *Composition with Red, Yellow, Blue and Black* 1921
(Composition)
oil on canvas
59.5 × 59.5 cm.
Gemeentemuseum, The Hague
cat. 312

114 *Tableau No. II* 1921–5
oil on canvas
75 × 65 cm.
Max Bill, Zurich and Ulm
cat. 308

115 *Composition with Red, Yellow and Blue* 1921
(Composition avec rouge, jaune et bleu)
oil on canvas
80 × 50.2 cm.
Gemeentemuseum, The Hague
cat. 311

116 *Tableau I* 1921
oil on canvas
96.5 × 60.5 cm.
Dr Oscar Müller-Widman, Basle
cat. 319

117 *Composition in White and Black* 1926
(Composition en blanc et noir)
oil on canvas
112.5 × 112 cm.
The Museum of Modern Art, New York
Katherine S. Dreier Bequest
cat. 405

118 *Composition I with Blue and Yellow* 1925
(Composition I avec bleu et jaune)
oil on canvas
80 × 80 cm.
Sidney Janis Gallery, New York
cat. 403

119 *Composition* 1921
oil on canvas
103 × 99 cm.
Private collection, Germany
cat. 316

120 *Composition III with Red, Yellow and Blue* 1927
(Composition III avec rouge, jaune et bleu)
oil on canvas
38 × 37 cm.
E. Elenbaas, Rotterdam
cat. 334

121 *Composition in a Square* 1926
(Composition dans le carré)
oil on canvas
51 × 51 cm.
Harry Holtzman, New York
cat. 331

122 *Composition with Red, Yellow and Blue* 1927
(Composition avec rouge, jaune et bleu)
oil on canvas
61 × 40 cm.
Stedelijk Museum, Amsterdam
cat. 364

123 *Fox Trot A* 1927
oil on canvas
diagonal 110 cm.
Yale University Art Gallery, New Haven, Conn.
cat. 407

124 *Composition with Red, Yellow and Blue* 1928
(Composition avec rouge, jaune et bleu)
oil on canvas
Morton Neumann, Chicago
cat. 336

125 *Composition with Red, Yellow and Blue* 1927

(Composition avec rouge, jaune et bleu)
oil on canvas
38×25 cm.
Sidney Janis Gallery, New York
cat. 366

126 *Large Composition with Red, Blue and Yellow* 1928
(Grande composition avec rouge, bleu et jaune)
oil on canvas
122×79 cm.
John L. Senior Jr., New York
cat. 367

127 *Composition with Red, Yellow and Blue* 1922
oil on canvas
42×50.2 cm.
Stedelijk Museum, Amsterdam
cat. 326

128 *Composition III* 1929
oil on canvas
50.5×50.5 cm.
Théodore Bailly, Montreux
cat. 346

129 *Fox Trot B* 1929
oil on canvas
44×44 cm.
Yale University Art Gallery, New Haven, Conn.
(Collection Société Anonyme)
cat. 337

130 *Composition in a Square with Red, Yellow and Blue* 1926
(Composition dans le carré avec rouge, jaune et bleu)
oil on canvas
102.5×102.5 cm.
Mr and Mrs H. M. Rothschild, Ossining, New York
cat. 404

131 *Composition with Black and Blue* 1926
(Composition avec noir et bleu)
oil on canvas
85×85 cm.
Philadelphia Museum of Art, Gallatin Collection
cat. 406

132 *Composition* 1929
oil on canvas
52×52 cm.
Mrs Marguerite Hagenbach, Basle
cat. 343

133 *Composition in a Square* 1929
(Composition dans le carré)
oil on canvas
Yale University Art Gallery, New Haven, Conn.
(Collection Société Anonyme)
cat. 342

134 *Composition with Red, Yellow and Blue* 1927
(Composition avec rouge, jaune et bleu)
oil on canvas
61.2×40 cm.
Stedelijk Museum, Amsterdam
cat. 364

135 *Composition* 1930
oil on canvas
Harry Holtzman, New York
cat. 351

136 *Composition* 1931
oil on canvas
50×50 cm.
Sidney Janis Gallery, New York
cat. 353

137 *Composition I* 1930
oil on canvas
50×50 cm.
Dr E. Friedrich-Zetzler, Zürich
cat. 352

138 *Composition with Yellow* 1930
(Composition avec jaune)
oil on canvas
46.5×46.5 cm.
Jan Tschichold, Basle
cat. 348

139 *Composition I with Black Lines* 1930
(Composition I avec lignes noires)
oil on canvas
41×32.5 cm.
John L. Senior Jr., New York
cat. 359

140 *Composition with Red, Black and White* 1931
(Composition avec rouge, noir et blanc)
oil on canvas
81×54 cm.
Mrs Charmion von Wiegand, New York
cat. 361

141 *Composition 2 with Black Lines* 1930
(Composition 2 avec lignes noires)
oil on canvas
51×50 cm.
Stedelijk van Abbe Museum, Eindhoven
cat. 360

142 *Composition IA* 1930
oil on canvas
70×70 cm.
Hilla Rebay, USA
cat. 408

143 *Composition with two Lines* 1931
(Composition avec deux lignes)
oil on canvas
diagonal 123 cm.
Stedelijk Museum, Amsterdam
cat. 409

144 *Composition D with Red, Yellow and Blue* 1932
(Composition D, avec rouge, jaune et bleu)
oil on canvas
42×38.5 cm.
Max Bill, Zurich and Ulm
cat. 355

145 *Composition with Blue and Yellow* 1932
(Composition avec bleu et jaune)
oil on canvas
Philadelphia Museum of Art Gallatin Collection
cat. 356

146 *Composition A* 1932
oil on canvas
55×55 cm.
Dr E. Friedrich-Seltzer, Zurich
cat. 354

147 *Composition B with Grey and Yellow* 1932
(Composition avec gris et jaune)
oil on canvas
50×50 cm.
Müller-Widman, Basle
cat. 368

148 *Composition with Blue and Red* 1933
(Composition avec bleu et rouge)
oil on canvas
40×33 cm.
Sidney Janis Gallery, New York
cat. 358

149 *Composition with Blue and Yellow* 1933
(Composition avec bleu et jaune)
oil on canvas
41×33.5 cm.
Dr Oskar Müller-Widman, Basle
cat. 369

150 *Composition with Blue* 1935
(Composition avec bleu)
oil on canvas
71×69 cm.
Mr and Mrs Harry L. Winston, Birmingham, Michigan

151 *Composition with Red and Black* 1936
(Composition avec rouge et noir)
oil on canvas
59×56.5 cm.
Sidney Janis Gallery, New York
cat. 377

152 *Composition* 1935
oil on canvas
56×54 cm.
Art Institute, Chicago

153 *Composition with Red and Blue* 1936
(Composition avec rouge et bleu)
oil on canvas
98×80.5 cm.
Felix Witzinger, Indianapolis
cat. 389

154 *Composition with Blue and Yellow* 1936
(Composition avec bleu et jaune)
oil on canvas
Harry Holtzman, New York
cat. 381

155 Mondrian's manuscript for the first issue of *Cercle et Carré*, Paris 1930
(see p. 251)

156 *Tableau-Poème* with Michel Seuphor 1928
colour lithograph
61.1×49.5 cm.
Michel Seuphor, Paris
(see p. 251)

157 *Composition with Red and Black* 1927
(Composition avec rouge et noir)
oil on canvas
56×56 cm.
Jon Nicholas Streep, New York
cat. 339

158 *Composition B with Red* 1935
(Composition B avec rouge)
oil on canvas
91.5×71.5 cm.
Helen Sutherland, London (?)
cat. 376

159 *Composition III with Blue and Yellow* 1936
(Composition III avec bleu et jaune)
oil on canvas
43.5×33.5 cm.
Kunstmuseum, Basle
Emanuel Hoffmann Fund
cat. 373

160 *Composition with Red* 1936
(Composition avec rouge)
oil on canvas
63×40.5 cm.
Mr and Mrs J. L. Sadie Martin
cat. 372

161 *Composition* 1935
oil on canvas
Private collection
cat. 389

162 *Composition with Red, Yellow and Blue* 1928
(Composition avec rouge, jaune et bleu)
oil on canvas
45×45 cm.
Martin Stam, Amsterdam
cat. 340

163 *Composition with Red, Blue and Yellow* 1930

(Composition avec rouge, bleu et jaune)
oil on canvas
48 × 48 cm.
Mr and Mrs Armand P. Bartos, New York
cat. 349

164 *Composition with Blue* 1937
(Composition avec bleu)
oil on canvas
79 × 80 cm.
Marcus Brumwell, London
cat. 395

165 *Composition with Yellow Lines* 1933
(Composition avec lignes jaunes)
oil on canvas
diagonal 113 cm.
Gemeentemuseum, The Hague
cat. 410

166 *Composition 2 with Red and Blue* 1937
(Composition 2 avec rouge et bleu)
oil on canvas
75 × 60.5 cm.
Ben Nicholson and Barbara Hepworth, London
cat. 394

167 Mondrian's studio in New York
On the easel *Victory Boogie-Woogie*

168 *Composition with Red* 1937
(Composition avec rouge)
oil on canvas
50.7 × 50.4 cm.
Philadelphia Museum of Art, Gallatin Collection
cat. 383

169 *Composition with Yellow, Blue and White* 1937
(Composition avec jaune, bleu et blanc)
oil on canvas
Private collection
cat. 393

170 *Composition with Blue and Yellow* 1937
(Composition avec bleu et jaune)
oil on canvas
55.8 × 45 cm.
Sidney Janis Gallery, New York
cat. 391

171 *Composition with Red and Yellow* 1937
(Composition avec rouge et jaune)
oil on canvas
43 × 33 cm.
Philadelphia Museum of Art, Gallatin Collection
cat. 390

172 *Composition with Blue* (unfinished) *c.* 1938
(Composition avec bleu)
oil on canvas
50 × 60 cm.
G. J. Nieuwenhuizen Segaar Gallery, The Hague
cat. 428

173 *Composition* (unfinished) 1938
oil on canvas
61 × 50 cm.
Harry Holtzman, New York
cat. 429

174 *Composition with Red* 1939
(Composition avec rouge)
oil on canvas
Harry Holtzman, New York
cat. 398

175 *Composition with Red* 1939
(Composition avec rouge)
oil on canvas
102 × 104 cm.
Peggy Guggenheim, Venice
cat. 399

176 *Composition No. 7* 1937–42
(Composition No. 7)
oil on canvas
Private collection
cat. 414

177 *Composition with Red, Yellow and Blue* 1939–42
(Composition avec rouge, jaune et bleu)
oil on canvas
80 × 72 cm.
Harry Holtzman, New York
cat. 416

178 *Rhythms with Black Lines* 1935–42
(Rhythme de lignes noires)
oil on canvas
72.5 × 70 cm.
Henry Clifford, Radenor, Pa.
cat. 396

179 *Composition with Red, Yellow and Blue* 1939–42
(Composition avec rouge, jaune et bleu)
oil on canvas
72.5 × 69 cm.
Donald O. Stewart, New York
cat. 415

180 *Composition with Yellow* 1935
(Composition)
oil on canvas
58.3 × 52.2 cm.
Galerie Beyeler, Basle
cat. 371

181 *Composition* 1939–41
Private collection

182 *Composition with Red, Yellow and Blue* 1936–43
(Composition avec rouge, jaune et bleu)
oil on canvas
60 × 55 cm.
Harry Holtzman, New York
cat. 412

183 *Composition with Red and Black* 1936
(Composition avec rouge et noir)
oil on canvas
102 × 104 cm.
The Museum of Modern Art, New York
cat. 388

184 *Composition with Yellow Square* 1936
(Composition)
oil on canvas
73 × 66 cm.
Philadelphia Museum of Art
Arensberg Collection
cat. 382

185 *Composition* 1939–42
oil on canvas
89 × 79 cm.
The Solomon R. Guggenheim Museum, New York
cat. 413

186 *Trafalgar Square* 1939–43
oil on canvas
145 × 119 cm.
John L. Senior Jr., New York
cat. 418

187 *Composition with Red, Yellow and Blue* 1935–42
(Composition avec rouge, jaune et bleu)
oil on canvas
99.6 × 51.3 cm.
Mr and Mrs James H. Clark, Dallas
(reproduction in Seuphor inverted)
cat. 387

188 *Composition* 1935–42
oil on canvas
102 × 51 cm.
Burton Tremaine, Conn.
cat. 386

189 *Composition* 1935–42
Private collection

190 Poster of the retrospective exhibition at the Gemeentemuseum, The Hague 1966
Illustrated with *Ill. 141, Composition 2 with Black Lines*

191 *Composition II with Blue* 1936–42
(Composition II avec bleu)
oil on canvas
61×61 cm.
Sidney Janis Gallery, New York
cat. 397

192 Max Bill hanging one of his paintings

193 Vasarely: *Manhattan* 1964
sculpture
Galerie Denise Renée, Paris

194 Fritz Glarner
Relational painting No. 70 1954
Galerie Louis Carré, Paris

195 Ben Nicholson *White Relief* 1939
Dr and Mrs J. L. Martin

196 *Place de la Concorde* 1938–43
92×93 cm.
Harry Holtzman, New York
cat. 419

197 *New York* 1941–42
oil on canvas
94×92 cm.
Private collection, New York
cat. 420

198 Mondrian holding his painting: *Composition in a Square with Red* 1943
(Composition dans le carré avec coin rouge)
oil on canvas
J. J. Sweeny Collection, New York
cat. 411

199 *Composition with Red* (unfinished) 1938–44
(Composition avec rouge)
oil on canvas
80×63.5 cm.
Harry Holtzman, New York
cat. 427

200 *Composition* (unfinished) 1939–44
oil on canvas
73×68.5 cm.
Harry Holtzman, New York
cat. 433

201 *Composition with Red, Yellow and Blue* (unfinished) 1939–44
(Composition avec rouge, jaune et bleu)
oil on canvas
71×71 cm.
Harry Holtzman, New York
cat. 432

202 *Composition. London* 1940–42
oil on canvas
82.5×71 cm.
Albright-Knox Art Gallery, Buffalo

203 *Composition with Red, Yellow and Blue* (unfinished) 1939–44
(Composition avec rouge, jaune et bleu)
oil on canvas
73×70 cm.
Harry Holtzman, New York
cat. 434

204 *New York City I* 1941–2
oil on canvas
119.3×114.2 cm.
Sidney Janis Gallery, New York
cat. 421

205 *Victory Boogie-Woogie* 1943–4
oil on canvas
126×126 cm.
Burton Tremaine, Meriden, Conn.

206 *Victory Boogie-Woogie c.* 1943
oil on canvas
diagonal 48 cm.
Harry Holtzman, New York
cat. 424

207 *Broadway Boogie-Woogie* 1942–3
oil on canvas
127× 127 cm.
The Museum of Modern Art, New York

208 *Broadway Boogie-Woogie* study 1942
pencil drawing
127× 127 cm.
Harry Holtzman, New York
cat. 422

Acknowledgments

We would like to thank all museum authorities who have given permission for their pictures to be reproduced, in particular: Gemeentemuseum, The Hague; Rijksmuseum Kröller-Müller, Otterlo; Stedelijk Museum, Amsterdam; Frans Hals Museum, Haarlem; Stedelijk van Abbe Museum, Eindhoven; The Museum of Modern Art, New York; Phillips Gallery, Washington; Art Institute, Chicago. Thanks are also due to Mr J. P. Smid, Director of Kunsthandel 'Monet', Amsterdam, for securing photographs of pictures in his gallery and private collection. Grateful acknowledgment is made to DuMont Schauberg Verlag, Cologne, for placing at our disposal considerable photographic material on the artist's work.

The following are translations of the manuscript for Mondrian's contribution to *Cercle et Carré* (*Ill. 155*, p. 167) and Michel Seuphor's text for the *Tableau-Poème* (*Ill. 156*, p. 168).

Not to concern oneself with form or with colour-as-form: this is the new plastic art.

Not to be too much dominated by the physical-natural: this is the new mentality.

To deal exclusively with relationships, creating them and seeking to balance them in art and in life: this is the beautiful task of today; to do this is to prepare for the future.

December 1929 PIET MONDRIAN

TEXTUAL

physical islet Seuphor under the wing of Mondrian
under the serious flags of neo-plasticism
flying the very pure banner

blessed release in art
act of hygiene
rally round the flag of rescue
of earnest when we see clearer
and let the flora wither under the neo gaze
and let the crumbling cease

the physical islet leaves the caverns
it dares build in the light
it lifts its head
where there is only the great blue
and the great grey and the great white
and the great black and the sun all fire
followed by synonyms happiness wisdom knowledge
and by joy . . .
which must not be confused

but it had to be thought of if I may say
to be already and not to choose and yet to choose
but contact had to be made
a long march and under the right sign.

16 May 1928 M. SEUPHOR

Index

L. P.-F. Léonard DANEL - LOOS (Nord)